GET A JOB IN FRANCE

A guide to employment opportunities and contacts

Mark Hempshell

How To Books

The information in this book is checked accurate at the time of writing. However, details are subject to continual change and readers must confirm these for themselves before travelling to France. When travelling it is essential to take out suitable travel insurance, and enough money to support yourself on arrival and to pay for your return home if you do not find a job or a pre-arranged job proves unsuitable.

British Library cataloguing-in-publication data
A catalogue record for this book is available from the British Library.

© 1993 by Mark Hempshell

First published in 1993 by How To Books Ltd, Plymbridge House, Estover Road, Plymouth PL6 7PZ, United Kingdom. Tel: Plymouth (0752) 735251/ 695745. Fax: (0752) 695699. Telex: 45635.

All rights reserved. No part of this work may be reproduced or stored in an information retrieval system (other than short extracts for the purposes of review) without the express permission of the Publishers given in writing.

Typeset by PDQ Typesetting, Stoke-on-Trent
Printed and bound by The Cromwell Press, Melksham, Wiltshire.

Preface

Around two years ago, when my first book on working in France appeared, the situation across the Channel was rather different to that which exists today. Although it had been possible to work in France freely for many years, fairly few foreigners were working there. The advantages of greater European cooperation were still very unclear. People knew they could work in France, but were not sure how, or even why!

Today the road ahead is much clearer. The **Single European Market** is in place. The ways of finding and getting a job have been opened up. Better still, the majority of would-be expatriates know why they want to work in France. And French employers are recognising the advantages of recruiting a European.

Attractive scenery, good food and cheaper property may be very valid reasons for going to work in France; but today's expatriates are very practical. They know that good wages and excellent career opportunities can be had in France. With a workforce only slightly smaller than the UK, extending your horizons to France almost *doubles* the number of vacancies for which you may be eligible!

British citizens can work in all the **European Community (EC)** countries, France inclued. As our nearest neighbour, though, and the country with which more British people are familiar (even if sometimes frustrated by the French character), France is one of the top choices of those seeking to put themselves on the international jobs market. France is now home to over 4.5 million expatriates!

In consequence, the number of people going to work in France can only increase over the next ten years or so, but the best and most numerous opportunities will surely be in the early days. The time to seriously consider the possibilities of working in France is most definitely now.

This book sets out to plot a clear and unmistakable route towards getting a job in France. I hope you find it useful and that, should you decide working in Paris, Nice, Brittany or the Dordogne is for you, it points the way to the job you want.

With particular thanks to the French Consulate, CIDJ, Institut Français, Manpower Ltd and DTI, among many other organisations, for providing accurate information for inclusion in this book.

Good luck.

Mark Hempshell

Contents

Preface 5

List of illustrations 10

1 Introduction to working in France 11

    What are the possibilities? 11
    The practicalities 11
    About the country 12
    Is it feasible for me? 13
    Step-by-step 17
    Case histories 17

2 How to find a job in France 19

    Using the UK media 19
    Career bulletins 21
    Using the French media 21
    The UK Employment Service 25
    The French Employment Service 30
    UK employment agencies 34
    French employment agencies 35
    Minitel 37
    International sources of jobs 37
    Finding unadvertised vacancies in France 38
    Advertising in French newspapers 41
    Other sources of job leads 44
    How do you secure a posting to France? 45

3 Applying for jobs in France 49

    Your qualifications in France 49
    How do the French think? 54
    Recruitment procedures in France 56
    How do you write your application? 59
    How do you prepare a CV? 62
    Handling application forms 67

	Interviews	69
	Checklist of key points	74
4	Working in France	75
	Residence in France	75
	Employment law and contracts of employment	76
	What should you do about disputes at work?	83
	Rates of pay and other benefits	84
	What are working conditions like?	87
	Trades unions and works councils	91
	Equality at work	94
	Where do you find out more?	96
	Checklist	96
5	Guide to French employment	97
	Does France need you?	97
	What job should you do?	98
	The main types of work available	98
	What are the main industries?	101
	Opportunities for casual work, holiday work and working exchanges	109
	Main types of casual and holiday work in France	112
	France by regions	118
	Checklist	120
6	Relocating to France	121
	Moving your home to France	121
	Learning the language	124
	Finding a home	125
	Social security in France	127
	Hospitals and health provision	130
	Money and banks	131
	Income tax	132
	Children and education	134
	Daily life	135
	Further help	136
7	Summing up	138
	A plan of action	138
	Step-by-step	139
	Further reading	140
	Books and directories	140
	Magazines and journals	141

Contents

Useful addresses	**142**
General alphabetical listing	142
Main French regional newspapers	143
Chambers of commerce	146
Embassies and consulates	146
Manpower branches (selected)	147
Paris employment agencies (selected)	147
Major employers in France	148
Main UK companies in France	150
UK employment agencies	151
Main ANPE offices	152
CIDJ offices	153
Glossary of French employment terms	**155**
Index	**157**

List of Illustrations

1. Map of France — 14
2. Examples of French job advertisements — 26
3. Using the French telephone directory — 32
4. How the ANPE is organised — 33
5. International sources of jobs — 39
6. Examples of Demandes d'Emploi advertisements — 43
7. The recruitment procedure — 58
8. Sample application letter in French — 63
9. Sample application letter in English — 64
10. How to address your envelope correctly — 65
11. Sample French CV — 66
12. How to decode the application form — 68
13. Specimen contract of employment — 78
14. Examples of salaries — 85
15. France's main nationalised companies — 100

1
Introduction to Working in France

WHAT ARE THE POSSIBILITIES?

In cultural terms, France can sometimes seem a long way from the UK. Language, customs, food and traditions are all very different—or exciting—and sometimes seem quite hostile. This should never be forgotten when seeking a job in France. However, it is also worth remembering that, in international employment terms, France and the UK have many more similarities than differences.

Industrially and commercially France and the UK share many key industries. Both have advanced First World economies. Both are very innovative countries, and leaders in their own particular fields. In both countries skilled workers, unskilled workers, professional people and executives do *identical* jobs every day, with merely a different cultural and language backdrop.

The two economies are also complementary. For example, while French industrialists are highly competent in manufacturing, British businessmen and women excel in providing high quality services. French research, development and design are strong, but financial and management skills are very much a British forte.

It is, therefore, only logical that both countries should cooperate more fully, in conjunction with our other European partners. Sometimes the barriers put up by differing languages, customs, food and traditions appear prohibitive. However, if we can deal with these successfully we are afforded access to excellent jobs which, in reality, are not that far removed from the jobs which exist in Britain.

THE PRACTICALITIES

Your rights

Under European Community (EC) law there is now absolutely no reason why a citizen of an EC member state should not just take off and go to work in another EC country, such as France. This right is central to the operation of the Single European Market (SEM), effective from 1 January 1993. It affords total freedom of movement of people, goods, capital and services between EC countries, free of taxes or restrictions of national law.

No restrictions
No work permits or certificates (other than those which also apply to French people) are required to get a job in France, or indeed any other EC country. It is your right to go there, look for work, and secure the best job you can.

This is a valuable right, but it is also a very practical one. It may be that you can find a job more easily in France. It may be better paid, more interesting and have better prospects. Now at last we are able to seek a job wherever we can be best employed, not just our home country.

Are there any drawbacks?
Some practical difficulties will always exist. These include different language, different qualifications, different experience and living in a different culture. The fact remains though that many of these problems are surmountable with effort. That done, there is direct access to almost *25 million jobs* which exist in France today!

The opportunities are various
You may wish to make a new home permanently in France, or you may be looking for a short-term, career-building experience. You may just want a holiday job, or you may even want to semi-retire. All these are possible.

ABOUT THE COUNTRY

- Fourth largest economy in the world;
- a country at the centre of Europe;
- high standard of living, still increasing;
- labour shortages possible in some sectors, though persistent unemployment is a threat.

Most observers agree that the expatriate employment scene in France is set fair. After a troubled start to the 1980s—resulting in the implementation of a series of economic austerity measures in 1983—the economy has grown steadily, especially since 1986.

France has the fourth largest economy in the world, smaller only than Japan, the USA and Germany. It is ahead of both the UK and Italy, although growth in the 1980s was greater in both these competitor countries.

France is now well poised to take advantage of the Single European Market. Not only is the geographical position favourable, but the Government strongly supports industry. Awareness of the advantages of the Single European Market is high, though many French manufacturers are unused to having their markets attacked by foreign competitors.

France continues to enjoy a rising standard of living; there are some suggestions that it is now higher than the country can afford.

- Typical wages are substantially higher than in the UK;
- living costs are marginally lower;
- taxes (in particular social security costs) are still regarded as a burden.

Early reports suggest a shortfall in some classes of personnel in the future, especially among executive and professional people. This is due to a traditionally elitist educational and career structure which has starved French industry of competent, forward-thinking managers. Recruiting from abroad is both filling the void and helping companies to gain a foothold in foreign markets.

Having said this, unemployment has become a worrying problem over the last two years. French unemployment has traditionally been modest, but in the 1980s failed to reduce much even when other countries achieved substantial reductions.

It is estimated that unemployment will shortly be 15 per cent. However, well qualified and experienced expatriates are unlikely to be adversely affected.

IS IT FEASIBLE FOR ME?

Unlimited, or largely unlimited, access to the French jobs market means that there is no reason why anyone cannot look for a job in France. However, it is important to qualify this right. Although there are no official requirements there are some important basic qualities which ideally you should possess if you are to succeed:

- Skills: Do you have a definite skill to offer? This is as important in France as anywhere.

- Qualifications: Formal qualifications are highly desirable in France. More people have vocational qualifications than in the UK and some fields are closed to the unqualified, no matter how competent they are. (Many UK qualifications are acceptable.)

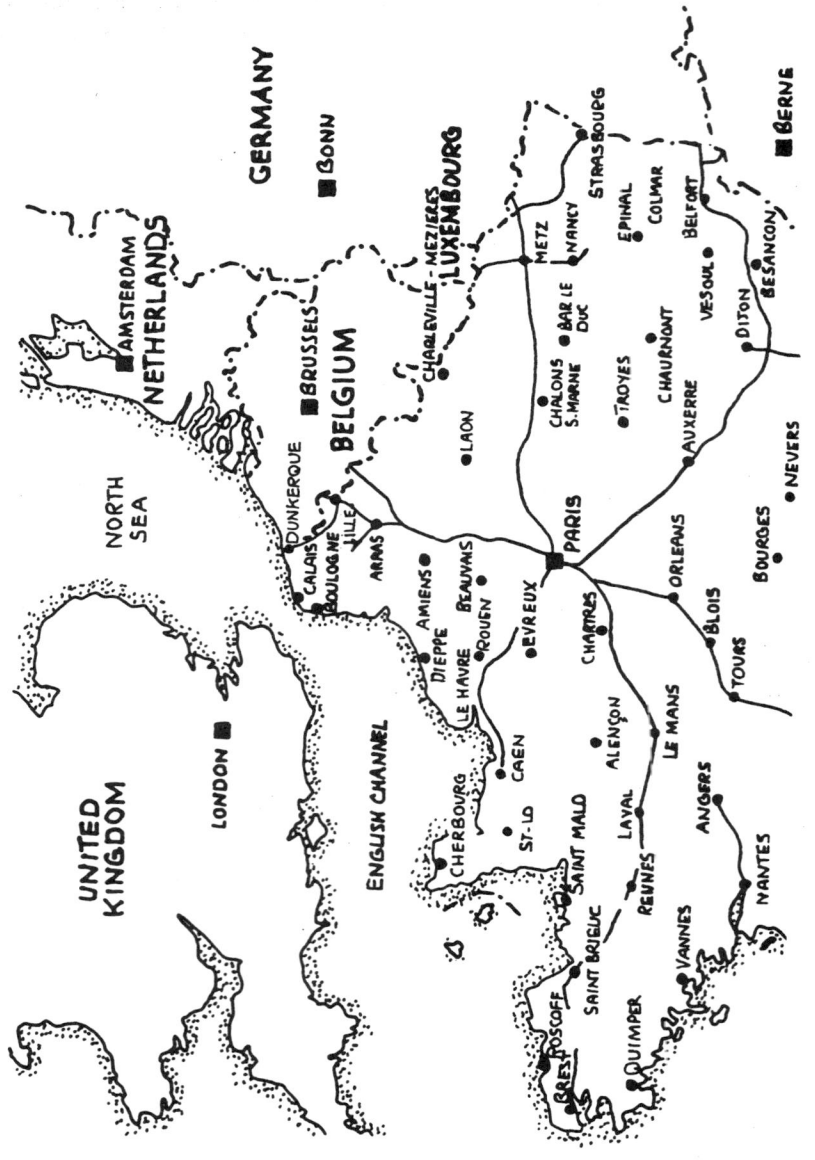

Fig. 1. Map of France.

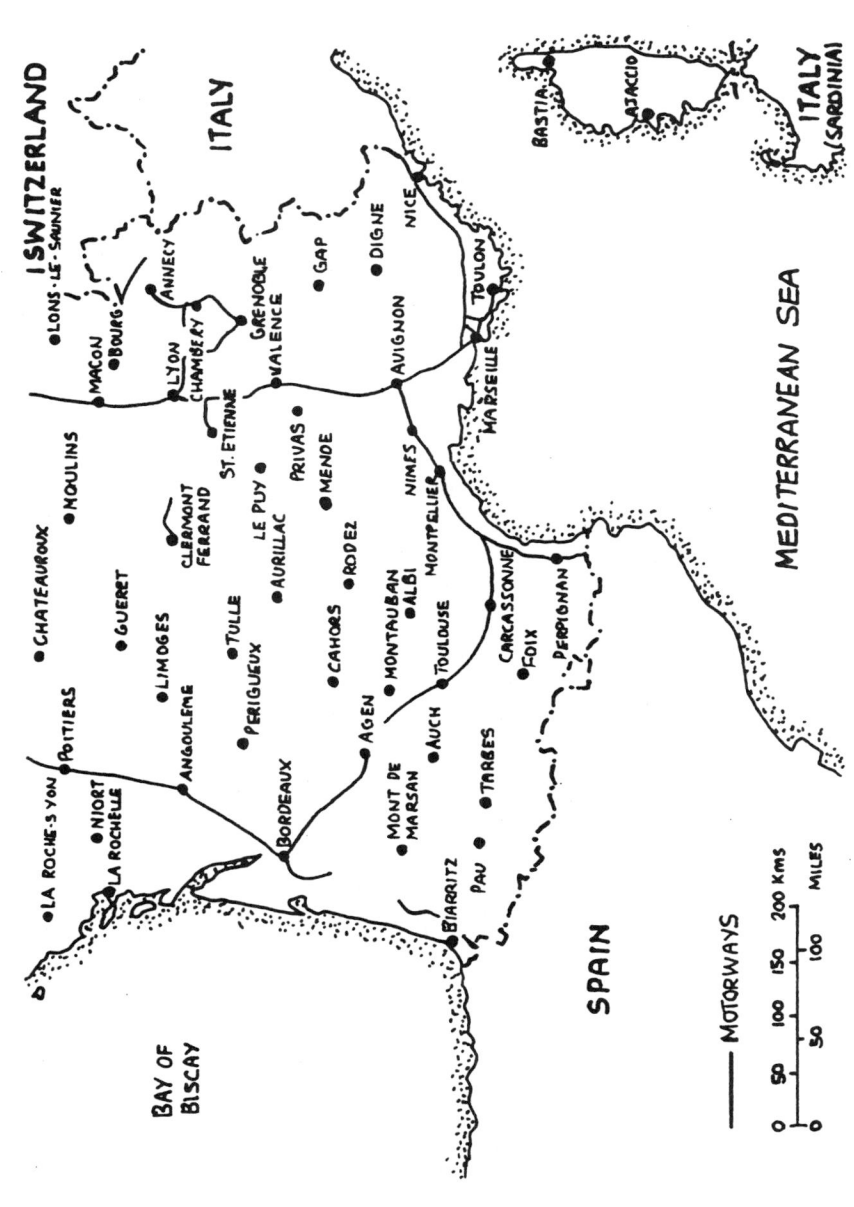

- Experience: As necessary as anywhere. The French value experience and maturity, perhaps more than the UK does.

- Language: To succeed you will need to speak French or be prepared to learn it. The French are protective of their language and frown on the spread of foreign languages. There are only a few very jobs where you could manage without.

- To like France! In many places it is unnecessary to like the country in order to succeed there career-wise, but you won't really be happy in France unless you do. If you hate garlic and 2CVs then you might have difficulty making headway in France!

Never choose France just because it happens to be our nearest neighbour, or because it offers an interesting way of life, or just because it offers good wages or career opportunities. All of these are very valid reasons, but above all choose France because you like it!

Finally, consider that although you can work quite legally in France, there is bureaucracy, discrimination, unemployment and competition for jobs just as anywhere else. And just as in the UK, some jobs are boring, dirty and underpaid too.

The pros and cons

Pros
- Shortage of personnel in some spheres.
- Foreign personnel are becoming more sought after.
- Higher rates of pay (typically).
- Living costs are generally moderate.
- Some types of staff (eg teachers) have more status in France.
- Much importance placed on training and career development.
- Some sectors of French industry are European or world leaders.

Cons
- Good knowledge of French is essential.
- National qualifications differ (though some are now considered equal in all EC countries).
- Your training and/or experience will be very different from that of your French counterparts.
- French employers may discriminate against foreign applicants.
- Unemployment and intense competition for jobs exist in some parts of France and some types of work.
- Some of the industries that are advanced in the UK are less

developed, less prestigious and less well paid in France.
- The right contacts and background are vital to obtain some top jobs. Foreigners may find this an invisible barrier.
- The recruitment network is not as advanced or efficient as in the UK.

STEP-BY-STEP

1. Decide what job(s) you wish to do.

2. Decide which areas you prefer/are most appropriate.

3. Consider which methods of application are most suitable in the circumstances.

4. Research sources of vacancies. Keep a running list.

5. Make applications.

6. If unsuccessful return to stages 1, 2 or 3.

7. Before accepting any job offer check out practicalities of daily life: finding a home, health care, education, etc.

8. Accept job and travel to France.

CASE HISTORIES

Marion Churchill
Age: 23
UK location: Dorset
Trade/profession: Personal Assistant (PA)
Qualifications: O and A levels, fluent in French
Wanted to move to: Preferred Brussels, Belgium
Wanted to do: Work for EC Commission
Eventually moved to: Nancy
Eventually did: PA to Export Director
Pay/conditions: FF160,000/year plus health benefits. Permanent contract.

John Powers
Age: 35
UK location: Yorkshire
Trade/profession: Textile plant manager

Qualifications:	O, A levels and professional qualifications; speaks some French
Wanted to move to:	Any part of France
Wanted to do:	Work in textile industry
Eventually moved to:	Lyon
Eventually did:	Development Manager with small family business
Pay/conditions:	FF280,500/year, plus health benefits, housing assistance. Hired on three-year contract to advise on expansion of the business to serve the US market.

Jeremy Milner

Age:	19
UK location:	Leeds
Trade/profession:	Student
Qualifications:	None relevant; speaks no French
Wanted to do:	Holiday work in France
Worked in:	Paris, Monaco and Sète (a permit is needed to work in Monaco)
Did:	Worked in fast food outlet, hotel and on a camp site
Pay/conditions:	Earnings from work paid for the entire trip, returned home with £64 profit!

Tony Jackson

Age:	29
UK location:	London
Trade/profession:	Advertising business
Qualifications:	Degree
Wanted to move to:	Paris
Wanted to do:	Work in French advertising industry
Eventually moved to:	Paris
Eventually did:	Account Director, marketing consultancy, working on UK and US accounts.
Pay/conditions:	FF320,000/year.

2
How to Find a Job in France

As in many European countries, the recruitment network in France is not as well developed as that in the UK. Firstly, there are fewer reliable ways of finding out about vacancies. Secondly, the methods that do exist are rarely as efficient as in the UK. For example, private recruitment agencies are restricted by law.

One important feature of the French employment market is the value of contacts, such as from school, university or previous employment. The 'old boy network' is very much alive and functioning in France. Those without the right contacts or academic history will find it harder to get jobs, especially the top jobs. Expatriates should try to make use of **networking**, but this cannot be expected to be easy.

This chapter will discuss all the methods of finding out about vacancies in France. It is advisable to use as many as possible, though not all are suitable for every type of job. Also, great importance should be attached to tracking down *unadvertised* vacancies, in addition to looking for vacancies which are being promoted. Consideration is given to this at the end of the chapter.

USING THE UK MEDIA

Which newspapers to use

The number of French vacancies appearing in the UK press is still fairly small. It will only ever account for a very small proportion of the available vacancies, but some do appear. It is worth keeping an eye out for them as these are usually jobs for which native English speaking is an essential requirement.

Advertisements mainly appear in the quality national newspapers; hardly ever in the regional press. The best newspapers to use are those with a specialist section devoted to a given type of vacancy on each day of the week, for example 'Media' *Guardian* on Mondays.

Newspapers to look at, in order of value, include:

- The *Guardian* (especially the 'Europe' section on Fridays)
- The *Independent* and *Independent on Sunday*
- *The Times* and *Sunday Times*
- The *Daily Telegraph* and *Sunday Telegraph*
- The *Financial Times*
- The *European* also features a small number of vacancies.

And to a lesser extent:

- The *Daily Express* and *Sunday Express*
- The *Daily Mail* and *Mail on Sunday*

Types of job on offer
The jobs on offer in France in the UK press are mostly executive and professional vacancies. Very few skilled trade vacancies appear, and there are never any unskilled vacancies.

The areas of business covered are engineering, science and technology, banking and finance, computing, electronics, advertising, publishing, media, secretarial and tourism. Few vacancies outside these fields appear.

Which professional journals to use

A number of professional journals which are based in the UK now carry French vacancies. This is usually the case where the journal has world importance. For example, *Flight International* magazine is published in English in the UK but circulates around the world and from time to time may have vacancies in France.

Professional journals are only likely to be suitable if you have existing experience and qualifications in a particular specialist field. Most of the jobs advertised in this way will demand them anyway. Usually, it will be necessary to speak French but, if a vacancy is being advertised in English, this may be unnecessary: your skills or qualifications are more sought after.

How to locate professional journals
Research will need to be done if you do not already know of all the journals which apply to your trade or profession:

1. Visit your nearest main library. Details of most professional journals can be found in *Benn's Media Guide Europe*.

2. Inspect back copies of the appropriate journals. (It is often necessary to ask the librarian as back copies may be kept in the archives.)

3. Quick check! Does this journal regularly carry vacancies in France, for which I am qualified to apply?

4. If so: Consider taking out a subscription to the relevant journal.

CAREER BULLETINS

There are now a number of career bulletins and overseas employment newsletters which can be used to track down vacancies abroad. Currently, the number of French vacancies advertised is quite small, but it may be worth examining some of them to see if a subscription would be worthwhile. If asked most of the publishers would send you a back issue for this purpose. Most are available by subscription only and some of the executive bulletins, offering the higher-grade jobs, are very costly.

Some bulletins to consider are:

UK

- *The Expatriate*, 56A Rochester Row, London SW1P 1JU. Tel: (081) 761 2575.
- *Home and Away*, Expats International, 29 Lacon Road, London SE22 9HE. Tel: (081) 299 4986.
- *Overseas Jobs Express*, PO Box 22, Brighton BN1 6HX. Tel: (0273) 440220.
- *Nexus Expatriate Magazine*, International House, 500 Purley Way, Croydon, Surrey CR0 4NZ. Tel: (081) 760 5100.
- *Executive Post*. Available from your local **Professional & Executive Recruitment (PER)** office.
- *Connaught Executive Bulletin*, 32 Savile Row, London W1X 1AG. Tel: (071) 439 0076.

France

- *Courier Cadre*, 8 rue Duret, 75783 Paris.
- *ICA Executive Search Newsletter*, 3 rue d'Hauteville, 75010 Paris.
- *1,000 Pistes de Jobs*, 27 rue de Chemin-Vert, 75543 Paris.

USING THE FRENCH MEDIA

Newspapers

As in most other countries the newspapers in France are a major source of job vacancies. Subject to the language barrier they can be used to find jobs quite successfully. However, if a job is advertised in French, in a French newspaper, it usually follows that you will need to speak fluent French.

It is particularly important to respond quickly to advertised vacancies in France, whether you are located in France or in the UK. Vacancies which call for a phone-in application are often filled in hours. If located in the UK at the time, it may be better to limit your search to vacancies which ask for write-in applications.

Which newspapers to use
There are very few national newspapers in France, unlike the UK where national newspapers are considered very important. Instead there are Paris newspapers which happen to circulate nationally. These can be used but carry very few vacancies.

In France, the regional and local newspapers are much more important and are the best source of job vacancies. There are also local papers and freesheets in many areas.

The main national (Paris) newspapers for vacancies are:

- *France-Soir*
- *Le Monde*
- *Les Echos* (business/financial).

The main regional daily newspapers include:

- *Sud-Ouest* (Bordeaux)
- *La Montagne* (Clermont-Ferrand)
- *La Voix du Nord* (Lille)
- *Le Progrès* (Lyon)
- *Lyon Matin* (Lyon)
- *Le Méridional* (Marseille)
- *Le Provençal* (Marseille)
- *Midi Libre* (Montpellier)
- *Presse-Océan* (Nantes)
- *Nice Matin* (Nice)
- *Ouest-France* (Rennes)
- *Paris-Normandie* (Rouen)
- *Dernières Nouvelles d'Alsace* (Strasbourg)
- *La Dépeche du Midi* (Toulouse)

The International Herald Tribune, Paris edition, may also have some suitable French vacancies.
Paris office: 181 ave Charles-de-Gaulle
  92521 Neuilly. Tel: 1 46 37 93 00.
London office: 103 Kingsway
  London WC2 0HJ. Tel: (071) 242 6593.

Addresses for the main French newspapers are given on page 143.

English language newspapers
There are a small number of English language newspapers circulating in France. A few vacancies may be carried, but they could also be used to advertise Situations Wanted (see page 41). The main ones are:

- *France Telegraph*, 7 place d'Armes, 24920 Montignac. Tel: 53 50 52 23.
- *The News*, 24500 Eymet. Tel: 53 52 76 16.
- *The Riviera Reporter*, 35 ave Howarth, 06110 Le Cannet. Tel: 93 45 77 19.

How to obtain French newspapers
Some of the main French newspapers can be bought, same or next day as published, at major newsagents in the UK. If the newspaper you require is not on display it can often be ordered. As the cost is typically 80p–£1 per copy it is important to check first if the vacancies are likely to be suitable, before placing a regular order.

Alternatively, contact the newspaper you require direct in France and place a subscription. Most will accept payment by credit card, thus making paying fairly easy. The cost of a subscription may seem high, but on a daily basis should not work out much more than the average UK quality daily newspaper. For example, a one-year subscription to *France-Soir* (Tel: 1 40 01 84 53), mailed to the UK, currently costs FF1,870.

What sort of jobs are available?
All kinds and grades of job are offered in the French newspapers, but it depends on the status of the newspaper as to whether they are unskilled, skilled, executive or professional. *France-Soir*, for example, carries mostly unskilled or semi-skilled vacancies. Some of the regional morning newspapers have a much better selection of executive vacancies.

French professional journals

French professional journals are a good source of vacancies, but as with UK profesional journals they generally only offer opportunities for those with specialist skills and qualifications. Within this, however, there are executive, professional and skilled worker vacancies. Your UK qualifications may well be acceptable to the French employer (see page 49). However, such vacancies will invariably require applicants to speak good French.

How to locate the journals
French professional journals can be located by checking in *Benn's Media Directory Europe* and then contacting the publishers direct. Ask for a sample copy of the magazine to see if suitable vacancies are likely to arise. If so, they can then be obtained on subscription.

A selection of professional journals
As in the UK, French journals tend to specialise across separate sectors of business and commerce. Some of the main journals are:

- *Publi 10* (advertising and media)
- *Agriculture* (agriculture)
- *AMC-Moniteur* (architecture)
- *Le Journal de l'Automobile* (motor industry)
- *L'Aéronautique et l'Astronautique* (aerospace)
- *Banque/Bancatique* (banking/finance)
- *L'Actualité Chimique* (chemical industry)
- *Radiodiffusion et Télévision* (broadcasting)
- *Travaux* (civil engineering)
- *Electronique* (electronics)
- *Les Marches* (food and produce distribution)
- *Mines et Carrières* (mining and quarrying)
- *L'Actualité Juridique – Propriété Immobiliere* (property)
- *L'Industrie Textile* (textiles)
- *L'Antenne* (freight)
- *L'Echo Touristique* (tourism)

How to read French job advertisements
Language apart, French job advertisements are not dissimilar to those in the UK in their presentation. Any good French-English dictionary can be used to translate the important terms.

You will find job advertisements under a section headed along the lines of:

- Carrières et Emplois, or
- Offres d'Emploi

Jobs are also found in the classified sections: Annonces Classées.

As in the UK the status and salary of the job are often related to the size of the advertisement!

All advertisements clearly state the post involved and the location of the job. This may not be the same as the area in which the job is being advertised or to which the response should be sent.

How to Find a Job in France

In most cases the body of an advertisement can be split down into four sections:

1. About this company: Notre Activité. A (usually quite grand) description of the company involved.
2. What this job involves: Votre Mission. In other words don't bother to apply if you cannot do this!
3. About you: Vous Avez.... Criteria which you must fit if you are to apply.
4. The package: Nous Vous Offrons. Why come and work for us?

Note that job advertisments very rarely state a salary. In many you must state what you want.

Details of how to respond are usually very clearly given: Se Présenter or Se Prés. – call in person. If a written reply is requested the elements required (CV, Lettre, Photo) will be clearly stated.

Note whether the advertisement has been placed by the employing company or a recruitment consultancy (identified by Recrutement or Ressources Humaines in the company name).

Some types of work
- Comptable: Accountant/book-keeper
- Chauffeur: Driver
- Secrétaire: Secretary
- Dactylo: Typist
- Sténodactylo: Shorthand typist
- Dessinateur: Design/draughtsman
- Magasinier: Warehouseman
- Electricien: Electrician
- Personnel hôtelier: Hotel staff
- Vendeur: Salesman/shop assistant
- Directeur: Director/manager
- Gérant: Manager
- PDG (Président Director Général): Chairman/chief executive.

THE UK EMPLOYMENT SERVICE

About EURES
It is possible to use the **UK Employment Service** in order to find vacancies which have been notified to the state employment service in France, which is called **ANPE**. Links are now well established so that

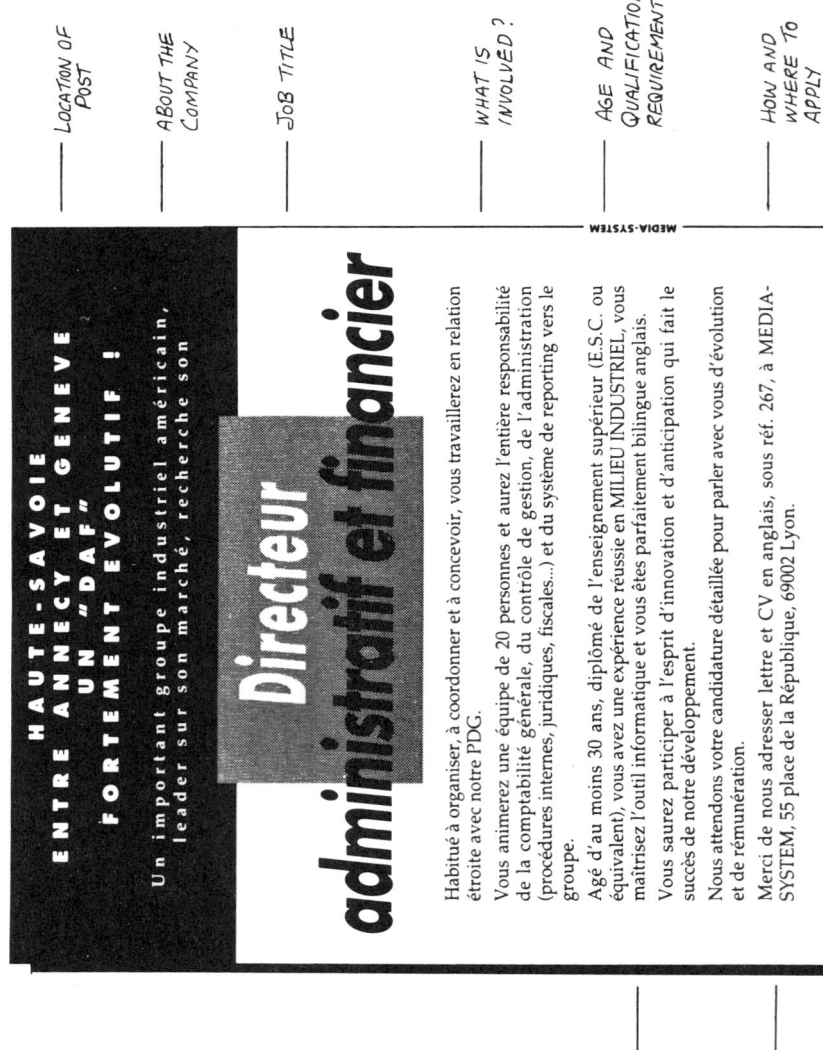

Fig. 2. Examples of French job advertisements

GROUPE AMERICAIN
recherche pour son Directeur administratif et financier

SECRETAIRE ASSISTANTE

— THE COMPANY

— THE JOB

PROFIL
- 35 ans minimum,
- bilingue anglais,
- maîtrise parfaite de la bureatique WORD 5, Lotus 1, 2, 3

LIBRE RAPIDEMENT

Motivation disponibilité, flexibilité et esprit d'initiative sont vos atouts

Vous souhaitez valoriser une expérience réussie de 5 ans minimum à un poste similaire en PME

— YOUR QUALIFICATIONS AND QUALITIES

MISSION
Secrétariat, relation avec siège, budget, gestion du personnel, reporting.

— WHAT IS INVOLVED

Nous vous offrons un salaire motivant dans un cadre agréable au sein d'une équipe performante.

— WHY WORK FOR US?

Merci d'adresser votre dossier complet (CV, photo, lettre de motivation et prétentions) sous réf. 23942 à EUROMESSAGES, BP 80 92105 Boulogne CDX, ou déposez votre cand. par Minitel 3616 EUROMES code 23942

— HOW AND WHERE TO APPLY

36 16 EUROMES

Restaurant chez Françoise aérogare des Invalides
PARIS 7e
recherche
JEUNE CHEF DE RANG
(Hme ou Fme)
JEUNE CHEF DE PARTIE
sérieuses réf. exigées.
SE PRÉSENTER CE JOUR.

— THE COMPANY
— LOCATION
— THE JOBS
— HOW TO APPLY

IMPORTANTE SOCIÉTÉ DE SÉCURITÉ
recherche
pour région ROISSY
MAÎTRES-CHIENS
Pour Athis-Mons (91)
AGENTS DE SURVEILLANCE
avec véhicule.
Se prés. avec réf. à P.V.S.,
42, rue Louis-Blanc, Paris 10e
M° Louis-Blanc
TÉL. 40.05.04.42

— THE COMPANY
— LOCATION OF POST
— THE JOBS
— HOW AND WHERE TO APPLY

Madrange
JAMAIS LA NATURE N'A EU SI BON GOUT

— ABOUT THE COMPANY

Nous sommes une société agro-alimentaire de premier plan (700 MF de CA), leader national dans le secteur de la charcuterie haut de gamme. Pour faire face à notre fort développement, nous renforçons nos structures et recherchons un

— THE JOB

DIRECTEUR ADMINISTRATIF ET FINANCIER

— BASED LIMOGES

POSTE BASE A LIMOGES

— YOUR RESPONSIBILITIES

VOTRE MISSION : Sous l'autorité du Directeur Général ❑ vous contribuerez à l'évolution stratégique de l'entreprise ❑ vous prendrez en charge les attributions complètes de la fonction : comptabilité générale, gestion budgétaire, fiscalité, affaires juridiques, relations avec les administrations, les banques et les assurances, dossiers d'investissement et primes, gestion des ressources humaines.

— YOUR QUALIFICATIONS

VOUS AVEZ : ❑ 35 à 40 ans environ ❑ une formation supérieure : ESSEC, SUP de CO PARIS..., spécialisation FI + DECS ❑ une expérience significative dans une fonction similaire et de préférence dans l'industrie agro-alimentaire ou dans un groupe.

— WHY WORK FOR US ?

NOUS VOUS OFFRONS : ❑ un haut niveau de responsabilité ❑ la force d'une société solide en pleine évolution ❑ un cadre de travail très professionnel ❑ une excellente qualité d'environnement.

— HOW AND WHERE TO APPLY

Pour un entretien individuel avec la société le 30/07. Adressez ou télécopiez CV, lettre et photo à EUROMAN - 11, rue Heinrich - 92100 BOULOGNE. Fax : (1) 46.21.78.13 en indiquant la référence 6001 sur la lettre et sur l'enveloppe.

EUROMAN

PUBLIPANEL

you can actually get a job in France via your local **Job Centre** under the auspices of the **European Employment Services (EURES)** network.

The system operates to all other EC countries, but you can restrict selections just to France.

How the system works

The system works in two ways. Firstly, you can apply for jobs that are already being circulated in the system via the Employment Service's NATVACS/SUPERVACS. Do this by going to your local Job Centre. Jobs are also advertised on the Oracle service (page 241).

Alternatively, you can make a speculative application. In this case you do not apply for a specific vacancy but your details will be circulated to state job agencies in France (the ANPE), assuming any have expressed an interest in recruiting people with the skills you have. Registrations are held for six months only.

How to register

Registration for French vacancies is done at your local Job Centre by filling in two copies of the multilingual form ES13. However, the procedure is administered by the **Overseas Placing Unit (OPU)** of the Employment Service in Sheffield.

Limitations

It is important to realise that the EURES network is not an absolute link to all French jobs. Rather, it is a system for exchanging information about vacancies and available personnel. ANPE offices will only circulate selected French vacancies to EURES, and only consider UK applications with skills and qualifications that are in demand but hard to find in their respective area. Often they are only interested in using EURES to fill vacancies which have been impossible to fill by recruiting locally.

The system is best suited to those who have a sought-after skill or experience to offer. In fact, although executives and professional people can be recruited in this way, most vacancies appear to be for skilled workers and highly skilled tradespeople. EURES can rarely help the unskilled or semi-skilled. Finally, it is usually necessary to have language ability in French.

The OPU can give general guidance and advice but cannot help with arranging interviews, contracts and permits. Once contact is made with an employer your further application and interview etc must be handled alone.

THE FRENCH EMPLOYMENT SERVICE

About ANPE
The French state employment service is known as the **Agence Nationale Pour L'Emploi**, or ANPE for short. With 600 offices all over France this is a similar organisation to UK Job Centres, has a comparable role and works in a similar way. It is probably slightly less efficient than the UK Employment Service Job Centres.

The main difference is that ANPE is strictly the only agency which can handle permanent employment in France. Private agencies are technically not allowed to do this by law. As a result ANPE handles all vacancies, from executive to unskilled posts, unlike the UK Employment Service which largely handles only skilled and unskilled jobs.

How much use is ANPE?
Citizens of other EC countries have a right to use ANPE and to be treated in exactly the same way as French nationals: no better, but certainly no worse. However, reports are that this is not always the case and many people report discrimination, unhelpfulness and, in some cases, seemingly deliberately misleading information being supplied. That said, this is not untypical of European state employment services, with the possible exception of Germany.

Employers are required to notify their vacancies to ANPE but, as elsewhere, many never enter the state system. Therefore ANPE should not be considered to have an exclusive listing of every job in France.

The vast majority of jobs notified to ANPE never enter the EURES system, so a direct application will throw up many more vacancies.

Where to find ANPE and how to use it

Where?
ANPE has offices in every city and major town in France: over 600 in total. Their addresses and telephone numbers can be found in the telephone directory or *Yellow Pages* of the appropriate département (county) of France. Most large libraries in the UK keep French telephone directories. Look under the heading 'ANPE'.

In some places there may be several ANPE departments, each specialising in different types of work. Temporary vacancies may be handled by a separate department. In some areas there are also part-time offices which recruit for casual or seasonal jobs. These are known as **Agences Locales et Antennes Saisonnières**.

How?
As a general rule ANPE offices will only deal with personal callers or

those telephoning from within the ANPE's local area. They will not deal with calls or letters from outside France; ANPE has no central agency to deal with foreign recruitment. Occasionally you will find a helpful official who will help over the phone from the UK, but it is rare. To use ANPE you need to speak some French. If you are fluent and look French then you are bound to get better service. English-speaking officials (or those who will admit to it) are very rare. The official line is that you need to speak good French in order to undertake the jobs offered by ANPE, but this is not necessarily the situation in the case of unskilled work.

How to register

It is preferable to go along and register at the ANPE office in the area of France where you wish to work. If you are prepared to consider jobs in several areas then register at several offices; the system, though national, is not well geared to finding vacancies in other parts of France, especially if they are in other départements or regions.

ANPE will require a permanent address, and may also ask to see a passport or **Carte de Séjour** (although technically this cannot be granted until you have found a job and applied for residence—see page 75).

ANPE will contact you directly if they have any suitable vacancies. You may also be called in from time to time and offered counselling (which may actually be quite negative and discouraging) and information on retraining, etc. However, it is as well to keep coming back and making a nuisance of yourself; as elsewhere those who sit and wait for a job to be offered will probably be unsuccessful.

All ANPE offices have a display area with computer print-outs of available jobs. Most people note down the contact details and then approach the employer direct. If you are plannng to stay in France for a while it is a good idea to travel round the various local offices and see what is on offer. For help in decoding the job descriptions see the earlier section on newspaper advertisements.

APEC and APECITA

In addition to ANPE there are two specialist organisations which can assist certain classes of job-seekers.

- **APEC: Association Pour L'Emploi des Cadres.** A cadre is a French executive who has attained a certain level of education and experience: it is very much an elite status.
- **APECITA: Association Pour L'Emploi des Cadres Ingénieurs et Techniciens de l'Agriculture.** This organisation advises cadre-status engineers and technicians. To the French a technician is an

**How to find a number or address
in the French telephone directory**

1. Each county or département has a telephone directory, so to find any number you must know what département the town is in.

2. The *white* pages are the alphabetical listings. The *yellow* pages are the classified trade directory.

3. The telephone directory is not a simple A-Z list. It is subdivided into an alphabetical list of towns, so to find any number you must know what town the address is in.

4. Within each town section is an alphabetical list of names—in that town *only*. Look up your required name in the usual way.

5. Names that are abbreviations are listed *either* under their full name *or* as if the abbreviation was a word. For example, the ANPE (Agence Nationale Pour L'Emploi) can be listed either under ANPE or Agence—not both.

6. Telephone directories can be accessed on **Minitel**. Printed directories will eventually become obsolete.

Fig. 3. Using the French telephone directory

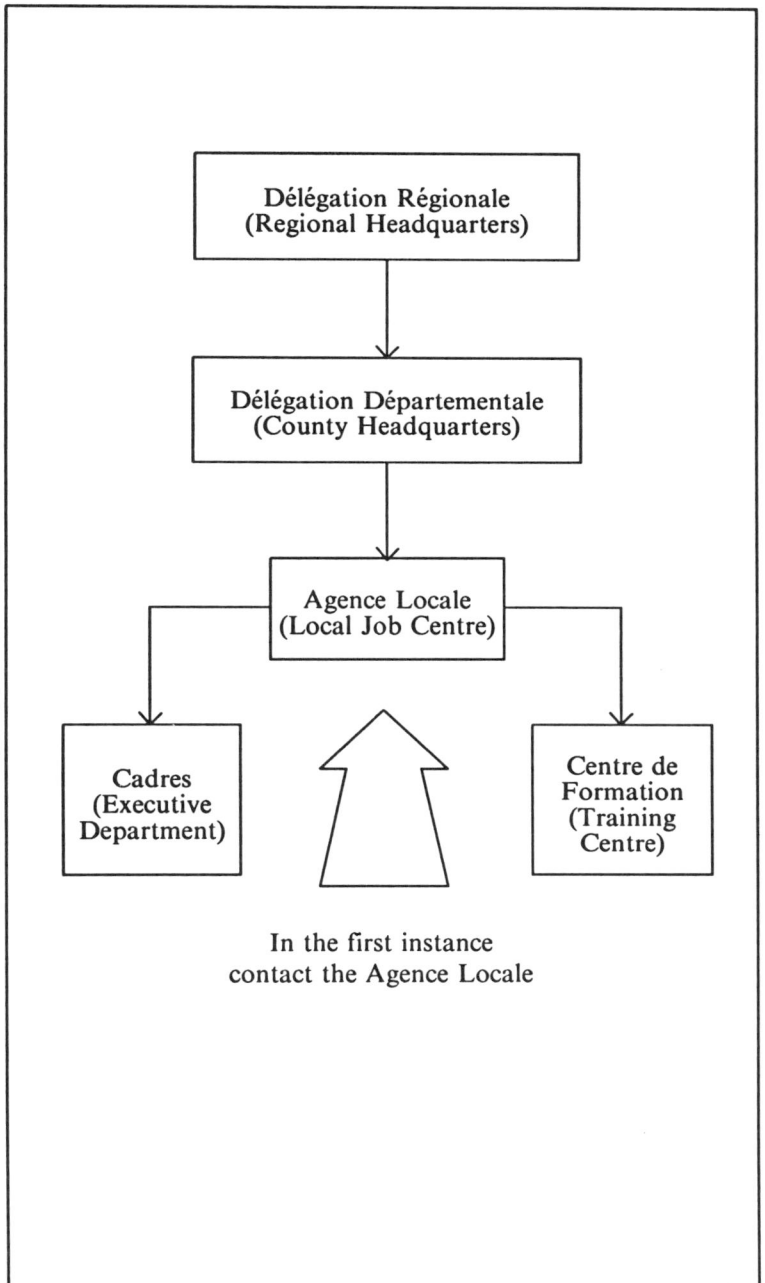

Fig. 4. How the ANPE is organised

engineer who does not qualify for cadre status

Regional contacts can be obtained from local telephone directories, but Paris contacts are:
APEC: 1 40 52 20 00.
APECITA: 1 48 74 93 25.

Further information
Further queries on the ANPE service can be directed to the head office. However, enquiries should be made in French.
ANPE
53 rue Général Leclerc
92136 Issy les Moulineaux
Tel: 1 46 45 21 26.
Addresses of some of the main ANPE offices are given on page 152.

UK EMPLOYMENT AGENCIES

UK employment agencies are increasing their links with France, and starting to deal with more vacancies in France and the EC as a whole. However, at present very few UK agencies have branches in France.

The vast majority of agencies dealing with France are retained by an employer to fill their vacancies. Few offer to find job-seekers a job, though most will hold details of well-qualified and experienced candidates on file in case a vacancy arises.

At present a hit-and-miss policy is the only one likely to stand any chance of success. Approach as many UK employment agencies as possible, advise them of your experience and qualifications, and ask if they are likely to have any suitable vacancies. One technique which has been successful is to forward *two* copies of your **curriculum vitae** or **CV**—one in English and one in French.

What types of job are available?
UK agencies tend to specialise in certain specialist industrial and commercial fields in France. They are also often on a temporary basis, or for fixed-term contracts, although this may eventually lead to a full-time job.

Generally, you require sound UK experience in one of the specialist fields to stand a chance of obtaining a job by this method. The ability to speak fluent French is almost always necessary.

Agencies mostly handle jobs in the following fields:

- secretarial
- electronics/computing
- media/advertising

- manufacturing
- teaching
- computing
- tourism
- construction/civil engineering
- nanny, au pair and domestic.

Finding agencies

Very few agencies advertise that they have jobs available in France, so an element of detective work will be involved. Agencies can be located by the following methods:

- Your local *Yellow Pages* directory.

- The **CEPEC Recruitment Guide.** Lists 600 UK recruitment agencies. Available price £21.50 from:
  CEPEC Publications
  67 Jermyn Street
  London SW1Y 6NY
  Tel: (071) 930 0322.
  Also at some libraries.

- The **Federation of Recruitment and Employment Services Ltd (FRES)** sell a *Yearbook* of members and will also supply a list of members with overseas placements.
  FRES
  36-38 Mortimer Street
  London
  W1N 7RB.

Addresses of some suitable recruitment agencies appear on page 151.

FRENCH EMPLOYMENT AGENCIES

Private employment agencies in France are largely restricted, by law, to operating as temporary employment bureaux. In reality, some of the jobs they offer turn permanent, or are for sufficiently long 'temporary' contracts as to be almost permanent.

Using a private employment agency is one of the very best ways of finding a job in France. It is preferable but by no means essential to have experience, qualifications or French language skills. The inexperienced and non-French-speaking stand a much better chance of finding temporary work, which may lead to a permanent job or a regular succession of temporary jobs, than a full-time permanent job.

What types of job are available?

Private employment agencies tend to specialise in certain types of work, often temporary by their very nature. These include:

- office and secretarial
- hotel and catering
- accountancy
- agricultural
- driving
- domestic
- technical
- professional
- general unskilled, eg work as a security guard or supermarket shelf-stacker.

Registering with an agency

Most French agencies are prepared to register foreign staff. Some experience a severe shortage of candidates, especially in summer (July and August) when permanent staff head off on their three- or four-week holidays and temporary staff are recruited to plug the gaps.

Registration is best done in France; very few agencies will take you onto their books while you are still resident in the UK. Many prefer you to have a French **residence permit** (Carte de Séjour) before accepting your registration. However, this is difficult to obtain if you do not already have a job—unfortunately, a classic Catch-22 situation.

In order to increase your chances of being offered a job, you may decide to approach several different types of agency and take a job which is not necessarily of your preferred type, until something more suitable becomes available.

Locating agencies

Employment agencies can be found in all the cities and main towns. There are several hundred in Paris, where agencies are much more used to recruiting foreigners than in the provinces.

Some of the agencies are small, independent, one-branch specialists. Others are chains which cover the country; the major names include **Manpower** and **ECCO**.

Details of employment agencies in your preferred part of France can be obtained from *Yellow Pages* directories. French *Yellow Pages* (called *Pages Jaunes*) are kept at most main libraries in the UK. Look under the heading Intérim. Addresses of some suitable agencies are given on page 147.

UK information
One of the largest private employment agencies in France is Manpower, with over 500 branches in all parts of the country. Manpower (UK) Ltd does not provide information on jobs in France, but is prepared to pass on the address and telephone number of the relevant Manpower France office in your chosen location.

Manpower (UK) Ltd
66 Chiltern Street
London W1M 1PR.
Tel: (071) 224 6688.

MINITEL

Minitel is a sophisticated information system, available in France, consisting of a computer VDU terminal linked to the telephone system. It is similar to the UK Teletext system but it is two-way in that it can be used to draw on information databases, make travel bookings and manage your bank account. There are over four million terminals now in use in France in both business premises and homes.

Job vacancies and general information on employment are available on Minitel, and it is worth checking the listings if you are able to visit France and have access to a terminal. The electronic telephone directory (**l'Annuaire Electronique**) is also accessible on the system.

Some companies will take your job application through the electronic mail facility of Minitel. If so, the **access code** will be stated in the advertisement.

INTERNATIONAL SOURCES OF JOBS

About the international recruitment network
As in many countries, jobs in France are sometimes available via other countries. Recruiting may be done outside France for various reasons. For example, employers in the north of France sometimes recruit French-speakers from Belgium. Highly skilled, technical staff are sometimes recruited or headhunted from Germany. Occasionally French employers recruit from Italy or Spain (where wages can be lower) in order to save on payroll costs. This is sometimes a reason why French employers recruit in the UK also.

At present, this network is still in the early stages and chances of locating a suitable vacancy through it are very slim. However, the system is bound to become more important in the early years of the Single European Market.

How to use the network

There is no reason why UK job seekers should not plug into this network. This is perfectly permissible and practical in the Single European Market. Vacancies can be located by referring to the usual recruitment channels, but in the relevant neighbouring country. The main restriction is the language barrier; usually you would need an outline knowledge of the language in the neighbouring country, as well as a knowledge of French—unless looking to the French-speaking areas of Belgium and Switzerland.

The chart in Figure 5 indicates how the various sources of vacancies can be used.

FINDING UNADVERTISED VACANCIES IN FRANCE

What is an unadvertised vacancy?

As in many other countries, not every job vacancy in France is openly advertised. Employers may often need personnel but not yet got round to advertising and searching for a suitable candidate. A more likely situation is where an employer could be persuaded to hire if the right person comes along. Part of the skill of using this system is to convince an employer that this person is you!

This system is particularly appropriate to France; the elitist educational system and executive cadre network mean that a majority of top jobs are handed down to personal contacts or a friend-of-a-friend.This percolates down to all levels of the job market. On a more practical basis the system works because French employers are not always well organised on the personnel front. They often need to recruit on the spur of the moment to cover for an unexpected situation.

Unadvertised vacancies are easiest to find for casual or holiday jobs. However, it is also effective for semi-skilled and skilled work, and particularly suitable for securing professional and executive posts.

Most French employers are receptive to being canvassed about unadvertised vacancies, especially if it allows them to negotiate a favourable (to them) employment package. A knowledge of French is preferable.

Locating potential employers

Locating advertised vacancies can be a hit-and-miss affair; it relies on the principle that finding and following up enough leads will produce sufficient chances of being offered a job. In actual fact, the success rate is usually no better than 0.25 per cent.

The following procedure is suggested:

1. Decide what type of job you can best do in France.

How jobs in France may be located in neighbouring countries

	Belgium*	Germany	Switz-erland†	Italy	Spain
Newspapers	✓✓	✓✓	✓	✓	✓
Professional journals	✓✓	✓✓	✓	✓	✓
Career bulletins	✓	✓✓	✓✓	✗	✗
State employment service	✓✓	✓✓	✗	✓	✗
Private employment agencies	✓✓	✓	✗	✗	✗

✓✓ Good potential   ✓ Slight potential   ✗ No potential

* French speaking Wallonia
† French speaking cantons

Fig. 5. International sources of jobs.

2. Decide what company is most likely to employ you.
3. Decide what areas have best potential/you would like to work in.
4. Locate sources of company data and addresses.

The following methods can be used to locate potential employers:

- Personal knowledge: List French companies you already know of. For example: Renault, Peugeot, Michelin, SNCF.

- *Yellow Pages* directories: French directories are available at major libraries in the UK.

- Chambers of Commerce: Chambers in France and the UK can be approached for advice, or asked for membership lists, revealing companies which trade in both countries. Further information on Chambers of Commerce is given later in this chapter.

- Trade directories: These are good sources of addresses. Ask at your local main library.

The *French Chamber of Commerce of Great Britain* recommend the *Kompass France* directory for this purpose. This is available for inspection at main libraries, and also the office of the Chamber in Knightsbridge, London. *Kompass France* is divided into four volumes: two are dedicated to a listing of products and services, the remaining two form a listing of business ('Entreprises' in French) divided between département numbers 1-66 and 67-95.

These sources of information can be used to build and maintain an address book of potential employers. Add new addresses as they are located and delete addresses as they are canvassed. Companies can be re-canvassed at regular intervals (every six months), even if they initially give a negative response.

Canvassing for unadvertised vacancies
Three methods of approaching potential employers are suggested:

- Writing letters: Recommended for executive and skilled vacancies. Write in French if at all possible; letters in English stand some chance of success but much less. Use a letter and CV package (more advice on this is given in the next chapter).

- Phone calls: Many French bosses do not excel at dealing with correspondence, so telephoning to sell yourself may be fruitful. You will usually need to speak in French *but*, if the job requires English-speaking ability (such as in tourism, secretarial work or nannying/au pair), this is often unnecessary.

- Personal calling: Making personal calls to offer yourself can be a difficult or disappointing business in France. It is only to be advised if you have a very thick skin! That said, it is by far the most successful method for obtaining casual work, where it might involve doing the rounds of all the shops, hotels, restaurants and the like.

Final tips
A crucial part of finding unadvertised vacancies is to get to know people and make contacts. Even if a particular person doesn't have a job to offer you they might make suggestions of where to try, or know a colleague who could use your services.

It pays to get to know your preferred area of France well, especially the local cafés, bars, restaurants, etc. In small communities the officials at the local Town Hall (**Mairie**), Chamber of Commerce (**Chambre de Commerce**) and Tourist Information Office (**Office du Tourisme** or **Syndicat d'Initiative**), and the local mayor and local police, may be interested enough to help. This is unlikely in cities, and not everyone is friendly, but such contact building and networking is an integral part of French business.

ADVERTISING IN FRENCH NEWSPAPERS

Using the Demandes d'Emploi columns
An alternative way of finding a job in France, which to some extent also targets unadvertised vacancies, is to place the equivalent of a Situations Wanted advertisement in a newspaper. In France these are found in the Demandes d'Emploi columns in most newspapers.

The chances of being offered a post by this method are similar to in the UK. That is, the proposition is realistic and does work but the possibility of ending up with your ideal job is modest.

Which newspapers to use
Any newspapers can be used. Within Paris, *France-Soir* has a good Situations Wanted column, mostly for unskilled and semi-skilled jobs. However, the regional and local newspapers are probably of more value. A list of the main ones appears on page 143.

Always check to see if the newspaper you intend to use has a

Demandes d'Emploi column, and if it is well patronised. Surprisingly, the more advertisements already appear there the better the chance of success. Newspapers without such a column can still be used but the chances of success will be much reduced.

Professional journals
These may also be used to advertise Demandes d'Emploi if you are looking for a specialist job and have appropriate skills and qualifications. A list of some of the main French journals appears on page 24 and a full list is available in *Benn's Media Directory Europe*.

How to place advertisements

Advertisements can be placed by contacting the newspaper direct. Many of them can take your ad by fax or phone, and take payment by credit card, thus saving on exchange difficulties. The cost at time of writing will usually range between FF5 per word and FF32 per word, although French newspapers usually sell space on a per-millimetre basis.

Alternatively, use an advertising agency. The cost may be slightly more but the advantage here is that they can not only place your ad, thus avoiding language problems, but advise on which newspapers to use and when to advertise. They may also be able to advise on the wording.

One such agency is:
Publicitas Ltd
517-523 Fulham Road
London SW6 1HD
Tel: (071) 385 7723.

Publicitas requests customers to send their wording exactly as required, for precise quotation of the cost. Payment is required in advance and it takes 10-14 days to place ads.

How to write your ad

Generally, advertisements should be short, simple and to the point. Advertising costs are invariably high, whether the circulation of the newpapers is high or low. A good technique is to write several versions and then cut down your word count. It is worth remembering that an English ad, when translated literally into French, can be 10-20 per cent longer.

Anglais ou Français?
It is crucial to make a positive decision on whether your ad should appear in English or in French. If the advertisement is in French it will

How to Find a Job in France 43

> Secrétaire sténo (anglais) remplacement ou partiel. 45-74-66-02
>
> J. H. 25a. diplomé finance cherche poste gestion-finance. Tél: 48-73-32-67
>
> J. H. 34 ans cherche place cuisinier dans brasserie. Libre. Tél. 44.73.42.38
>
> J. Hme 25 a., sérieux, bonne présentation, 3 a. exp. services relations publiques/ presse communication, rech. poste même secteur. 43-33-33-95
>
> Chef de rang, serveur, 40 ans. réf. bilingue, rech. pl. stable ou extra Paris banl. 42.37.48.88
>
> JNE HOMME cherche place PLONGEUR, NETTOYEUR Tél. 42.52.48.19.
>
> J. H. cherche place serveur dans pizzeria 6 ans expér. 43.21.51.11
>
> J. Fme, excellente présentation, niveau licence droit privé anglais, TTX, ch. poste auprès d'un courtier en Bourse. Tél: 42-03-11-41

- J. H.: Jeune homme. J. F. : Jeune femme. Young man/woman
- 25 a.: 25 ans. 25 years old
- Cherche: Looking for
- Sérieux: Serious/genuine/ambitious
- 3 a. exp.: Three years' experience

Fig 6. Examples of Demandes d'Emploi advertisements.

obviously be read by more people, and may impress as a courtesy to the potential employer. Take care, however, if your French is not fluent as it may give a deceptive impression of your language ability. If your advertisement is in English then it will stand out much better, but of course fewer people will be able to read it. French employers may take a dim view of advertisements in English—but it can be a job-winner if English speaking is a requirement of the job, for example, in tourism or secretarial work.

Some French newspapers can translate your advertisement but they will charge for this. To find a translator in the UK see Translators and Interpreters in your *Yellow Pages*.

OTHER SOURCES OF JOB LEADS

Assistance from professional associations

Professional associations can rarely find you a job in France, but it is always worth asking what help they can give. They can often:

- tell you about qualifications requirements;
- suggest potential employers;
- introduce you to foreign professional associations;
- introduce you to foreign professional journals;
- occasionally, they may know of actual vacancies.

If you do not already know of your professional association it can be located by looking at *Trade Associations & Professional Bodies of the UK* (Pergamon Press).

Assistance from embassies, consulates and chambers of commerce

The role of embassies, consulates and chambers of commerce is not to help people find jobs. However, they can sometimes provide useful information which can lead to contacts:

- French Embassy and Consulates: Have a leaflet of current information called *Employment in France*, which has particular emphasis on holiday work and exchange schemes.

- British Embassy and Consulates: Are not prepared to provide any assistance.

- British Chamber of Commerce in Paris: Can supply a list of members and has a directory available for purchase.

- French Chamber of Commerce in Great Britain: Publishes a *Franco-British Trade Directory*, providing details on member companies.

- French Chambers of Commerce in France: Every city and town in France has a chamber of commerce (chambre de commerce). Most will provide information on the local area, and lists of members in particular industries, especially if they consider you are a potential investor.

Addresses for embassies and consulates are given on page 146. Addresses for the national chambers of commerce, and those in the main French cities, appear on page 146. Local French chambers of commerce can also be contacted through their national association:
Assemblée Permanente des Chambres de Commerce et d'Industrie (APCCI)
45 ave d'Iéna
75016 Paris
Tel: 1 47 23 01 11.

L'Etudiant
L'Etudiant is an organisation for French students which, amongst other activities, publishes useful career guides. These provide a guide to career opportunities, mostly for students, but would also help young people. They are in French, but readable by those who have studied French to A level, or good O/GCSE level.

Titles include: *Les Métiers du Secrétariat* (Jobs in Office Administration) and *Les Métiers de la Gestion et de la Comptabilité* (Jobs in Management and Accountancy). Details of the guides can be obtained from:
L'Etudiant
27 rue Chemin-Vert
75543 Paris.

HOW DO YOU SECURE A POSTING TO FRANCE?

The possibilities and potential
Nowadays, most people wishing to live and work in France apply for a job direct with an employer there. However, an alternative is to initially seek a job with a company in the UK which has French connections and then secure a posting in France.

This method can be practical, as trading links between the UK and France are strong and set to increase as the Single European Market matures. French companies have aggressively been penetrating the UK market, especially in food products, utilities, etc. UK companies are keen to do the same, but have been slower.

Companies will rarely recruit with the promise or possibility that you may be posted to France, or indeed any country. On the other hand, few employees in any company are enthusiastic about being posted overseas against their will. If you demonstrate enthusiasm for it you may well be considered ahead of everyone else.

A plan of action

First step
If you are interested in a future posting to France then the first step is to seek a transfer of job to a company with strong French links. This should not be impractical if your skills and experience are appropriate.

Second step
Compile a list of prospective employers who have both strong links with France and are likely to employ people with your particular skill, experience and qualifications. Three sources are suggested for this purpose:

- The membership lists provided by the chambers of commerce, as discussed in the previous section.

- Cross-reference between trade directories to find companies with links in both countries. The *Kompass France* and *Kompass UK* directories are recommended for this purpose; ask at a main library.

- *The Personnel Managers Yearbook* (annual, AP Information Services Ltd) provides details of companies with posting potential.

Third step
Delete companies which are inappropriate for this purpose. For example, the companies distributing French cars in the UK are usually distributors or franchisees, not part of the French manufacturers as such. Even at this stage an exploratory telephone call to the company's personnel department may help ascertain if posting opportunities occur often, occasionally, or never.

Securing a job
The next step is to seek a job with your target companies in just the

same way as for any other job in the UK. In addition, do not simply wait for jobs to be advertised but pursue unadvertised vacancies. The chances of securing a post with one particular company are low, but they become realistic by targeting 300 or more companies in your preferred field.

During the process of applying for jobs and undertaking interviews, make it clear that should any future opportunities for posting arise you would be interested. For example, say or write:

'I am interested in any future opportunities for working abroad and have particular interest in working in France.'

If you have done your research well you will already have established that the company in question has French links. Few personnel officers would fail to notice and remember your interest as it could well make their life easier in future. Here they have a prospective employeee who is willing to be posted abroad!

Potential problems

Not many employers in the UK recruit staff with a guarantee or even a possibility of a posting abroad, although this is more common in France where executive staff are more likely to be offered the chance to work in Switzerland, or Belgium or even Francophone Africa. The time taken to secure your posting could be considerable; during that waiting period you will probably wish to keep looking for a job in France by direct application.

If offered a posting, remember that French salaries are often higher than those in the UK. You must be prepared to renegotiate your employment package. Some employers may offer a posting package which includes an increase in salary but which is still unsufficient.

Most companies will offer removal fees, school fees and assistance with the cost of housing. However, in France there is an increasing tendency for these to be fixed-amount contributions, rather than a blank cheque. Travel or visit-home costs are rarely offered since the costs of travel between the countries are not that great.

Special contacts

Those wishing to secure a job outside France, but with French connections, may wish to use two other sources of advice which are rarely used by foreigners, but appear to hold good potential for finding job leads.

Both these organisations are intended to help French nationals find a job outside France. In many cases, however, it seems there is potential to move to France at a later date, as many of the jobs are with French companies but outside France.

- *Migrations*
  3 rue de Montyon
  75009 Paris
  Tel: 1 47 70 46 84.
  This is a newsletter with job vacancies outside France for would-be French exaptriates.

- The Service International de l'ANPE
  3 rue Clairaut
  75017 Paris
  Tel: 1 46 27 70 57.
  Assists French nationals to find jobs abroad.

Both services are only suitable for those who speak fluent French.

3
Applying for Jobs in France

YOUR QUALIFICATIONS IN FRANCE

How important are qualifications?
Generally, qualifications are taken much more seriously in France than in the UK. Those without provable qualifications will find it much harder to get a job than in the UK. That said, it is often the paper value of qualifications which are important to the French employer, especially as regards university degrees.

If you have good qualifications it will not matter if they are not totally relevant to the job in hand; more importance is attached to attendance of schools and universities with a good reputation. Similarly, some occupations are effectively closed to those without specific qualifications, no matter how competent or experienced they are.

Your UK qualifications
Some UK qualifications are now officially recognised in France under systems introduced by the EC. It is always worth mentioning UK qualifications in your applications, although French employers are more prejudiced against foreign qualifications than those in other European countries.

Harmonisation of qualifications
Since January 1991 a number of UK qualifications have been accepted as valid in other EC countries, and vice versa. Over the last few years the **European Centre for the Development of Vocational Training (CEDEFOP)** has been working to devise systems by which many EC academic and most EC professional qualifications can be recognised across the community.

Two systems are in force:

- **Harmonised Training Directives.** Under the Harmonised Training system CEDEFOP has examined training courses all over the EC and decided which offer largely the same programme of training.

The qualifications this applies to are those for doctors, dentists, nurses, midwives, vets, architects, pharmacists, GPs and those in road transport.

- **First General System of Mutual Recognition of Qualifications.** Under this system training courses may have very different programmes, but the eventual qualification is considered of similar standard. The First System covers all qualifications obtained after three years' post-secondary study, plus all lesser qualifications in certain fields which are currently: manufacturing/processing industries; food/beverage industries; wholesale trades; intermediaries in commerce and industry; retail trade; wholesale coal trade; trade in toxic products; hotel/catering; insurance agents/brokers; transport/travel agency; hairdressing; some fishery; postal and telecommunications; recreational; community and personal services. More sectors are to be added.

Future plans

A **Second General System** is now drafted but may not be fully operational until 1 January 1995. This will make BTec and OND qualifications and many school qualifications recognised in France and throughout Europe.

Currently these qualifications may not be officially recognised, but some employers unofficially recognise them as equivalent to those obtained at a similar age in other EC countries (further details on page 52).

How to make use of your professional qualifications

It is not necessary to have your qualifications formally transferred to any other country. If appropriate they should be recognised as they stand. The way the system works is that your UK qualifications should be recognised as valid, by the appropriate professional body which supervises that trade or profession in France, to qualify for membership of their body. Qualifying for membership of that organisation, for example a French equivalent of the Royal Institute of British Architects, the Ordre des Architectes, allows you to operate that profession or trade legally in France.

For example
A midwife who has qualified in the UK is not ostensibly allowed to operate in France, as he or she will not have French qualifications in this subject. Actually, though, he or she can. This is not because their UK qualification is acceptable to French employers. Rather, their UK

qualification will entitle them to join the appropriate French professional body. By law this allows them to operate in France.

How to make use of your experience

The **European Community Certificate of Experience** exists so that your experience can be recognised and used to get a job in an EC country. If you have at least three to five years' experience in a particular field (it is not necessary to be qualified) you may qualify for a document which certifies your experience. A Certificate of Experience is useful where qualifications may be needed for a particular job in the EC but are not in the UK; the Certificate of Experience may be accepted instead. A case in point here is hairdressing; it is perfectly legal to operate as a hairdresser in the UK without qualifications, but in Europe hairdressers must be qualified.

Certificates are issued by the Department of Trade and Industry (DTI) in the UK. The process takes about four weeks and the fee is currently £50. The issuing authority will look at your experience, which you should be able to prove, at the relevant EC directives, and decide if you qualify for a certificate.

The trades which the Certificate of Experience currently covers are: manufacturing/processing industries; retail trade; wholesale trade; wholesale coal trade; hotel/catering; transport/travel agency; hairdressing; some fishery; postal and telecommunications; recreational, community and personal services.

Possible problems

Even where you are legally allowed to operate your trade or profession in France, an employer is still entitled to expect that you are competent to do the work and can speak the local language adequately. In some circumstances you can be required to undertake an aptitude test or period of supervised training.

Further information

Further information on the harmonisation and acceptability of qualifications can be obtained as follows.

UK
   The Employment Department
   Qualifications and Standards Branch
   Room E603
   Moorfoot
   Sheffield, S1 4PQ
   Tel: (0742) 594144.

Employment Service offices have an explanatory leaflet CVQE1, *Comparability of Vocational Qualifications in the EEC.*

Department of Trade and Industry
European Division 1
6th Floor
123 Victoria Street
London
SW1E 6RB
Tel: (071) 215 5000.

Also try your professional association.

France
Délégation à la Formation Professionnelle
50 rue de la Procession
75015 Paris
Tel: 1 48 56 48 61.

Also the appropriate French professional association (contact via your UK association).

The French system of qualifications

At school
Up until the age of 12 French students study a wide range of subjects at primary school (école primaire) and secondary school (either a lycée, similar to a grammar school, or a CES, similar to a comprehensive school). This leads to a basic qualification, the **BEPC (Brevet d'Etudes du Premier Cycle)**. Most schools are state run.

Going further
Next, a decision is made on a course of study to take students up to school leaving age. This is selected to meet the aptitudes of each student and the choice now limits their future career opportunities. The selection is broadly between academic, technical or practical study. There are several options, leading to very different qualifications:

- **Baccalauréat**: (In English, Baccalaureate.) A demanding academic examination, taken at age 18, or more usually 19. Similar to UK A levels.
- **Baccalauréat de Technicien (BTn)**: A baccalaureate in technical subjects.
- **Brevet de Technicien (BT)**: A vocational qualification at 18+.

- **Brevet de Technicien Supérieur (BTS)**: Similar to the OND qualification.
- **Certificat d'Aptitude Professionnelle (CAP)**: Basic vocational certificate.
- **Brevet d'Etudes Professionnelles (BEP)**: Skilled worker qualification.

The Baccalauréat
The Baccalauréat (known as the BAC) is a demanding qualification requiring rigorous study until an examination at 18 or 19. It can be taken with an emphasis on subjects such as the arts, mathematics, sciences and technical subjects. However, a BAC in sciences is much more prestigious than a BAC in the arts.

Universities
French universities are generally obliged to take all applicants who hold a BAC. As a result resources are stretched; a French degree is considered by academics as a lesser qualification to a UK one, though under EC regulations they are equivalent.

French degree courses can last between two and four years and lead to three qualifications:

- **DUT (Diplôme Universitaire de Technologie)**
- **DEUG (Diplôme d'Etudes Universitaires Générales)**
- **DESS (Diplôme d'Etudes Supérieurs Spécialisées)**

Elitist universities
The requirement to take all comers does not apply to the very top universities, known as the **Grandes Ecoles**, which are a race apart from the rest. They can set their own entrance examinations and hand-pick their students.

Applicants must be holders of a first-rate BAC and may have to undertake extensive further study to be accepted.

The system of Grandes Ecoles is put forward by critics as the very pinnacle of an elitist system which starves French industry of much talent and new ideas. Top jobs are usually only ever handed down through a network of old-boys of the Grandes Ecoles. But by the same token many jobs are closed to those without a BAC or a degree, no matter how good they may be.

How useful are your UK academic qualifications?
Whether or not all French and UK academic qualifications have been made equivalent at the time of moving to France, it is useful to know

something about French national qualifications and how they relate to UK qualifications. It is always worth mentioning UK qualifications in job applications and, if you can, stating what French qualifications they are equivalent to. Even if not officially accepted this can only serve to reinforce your suitability for the post in question.

A levels
Most French employers will accept that UK A levels are equivalent to a French BAC. However, it is generally believed by academics that the BAC is harder and that, for example, a BAC in science is only equivalent to A grades at UK A level in physics, chemistry, etc.

University degrees
Under EC regulations French employers must accept a UK degree as equivalent to a French one. In fact, for the reasons given earlier, the UK degree is most likely superior.

However, French employers seeking a candidate whom they expect to be a graduate of the Grandes Ecoles will not accept any UK degree as equivalent, although theoretically it is. They may insist on a UK PhD or MA qualification, and then from a UK university which they consider prestigious. Oxford and Cambridge are UK equivalents to the Grandes Ecoles.

It is customary for employers recruiting graduates to use terms such as 'BAC plus deux' or 'BAC plus quatre ans d'études' in their job descriptions. This indicates that only candidates with the BAC plus the indicated number of years of further study will be considered.

HOW DO THE FRENCH THINK?

The following sections will serve as a background to the situations which are likely to be encountered as you commence your application, undertake interviews and move towards your first French assignment.

Attitudes to employees

Employer-employee
The French employer/employee relationship is rather different to that in the UK and this should be borne in mind at the time of applying for work. Generally, employers are very demanding and can be quite dictatorial. This has been the case for many years and the worst excesses have required extensive legislation to mediate them.

In the workplace
The French attitude to the workplace is not a happy-family

atmosphere, where everyone works as a team and in which work and social life combine. This will come as a stark contrast to those used to working in a British office or factory floor. Employees are expected to work hard during business hours; but conversely, the time away from work is their own. For senior staff, taking work home is a sign of status; but others would rarely be expected to do more than that for which they are paid.

National variations
Attitudes vary across the country. Employers in the north are more old-fashioned and take a harder line; a fact reflected in the poorer industrial relations and worse strike record of northern firms. Those in the south are more relaxed and exhibit signs of being influenced by casual US business styles, though not totally.

Patriotism
The French tend to be naturally biased against foreign employees; less so against those in senior positions whose abilities they respect. It is true to say that, in many companies, foreign staff are largely recruited in order to 'pick their brains': to learn from foreign methods, or help the French company gain a toehold in a foreign market.

Generally, the foreign employee will need to attain higher standards of achievement than the French. Employees who can speak French well will always be better received; never believe the French colleague who says that he or she is happy to speak English. If you speak good French and admire, though not dote on, all things French, you can expect to earn a degree of admiration.

What do employers expect?
The expectations of the French employer are as different as the employee-employer relationship. In the vast majority of cases it is the foreign employee who must adapt to French expectations, not the other way round. Some particular points to consider are:

Intolerance
Employers demand high standards and are not always tolerant of those who do not perform or make mistakes. Rarely is any excuse adequate.

Obedience
An old-fashioned concept but still valid. Those at the top usually think they know best and do not appreciate their judgement being challenged. This is considered one of the fatal flaws of the French executive.

Participation (absence of)
Employers do not usually expect employees to be interested in the success of their company. Although participation is becoming more usual with the introduction of bonus schemes it is still the exception.

Hierarchy
Every French company has a hierarchy of staff; a good position in that hierarchy (such as cadre status) is a reward in itself. Company hierarchies and chains of command are not to be by-passed.

Currency
Employees are expected to remain current on the latest state-of-the-art of their trade or profession. Paid-for training in paid working hours may be provided for this purpose. It is only for this reason that the ability to speak a foreign language has become more desirable.

Contacts
At the higher levels, contacts and the right background are particularly important. The executive will be expected to develop contacts for the benefit of his firm, though the demands of socialising are not onerous.

Loyalty
Perhaps the most important quality expected. Clauses demanding loyalty, secrecy and providing for fidelity may be incorporated in many contracts of employment. French companies are jealous of their secrets (which actually may not be secrets at all!).

RECRUITMENT PROCEDURES IN FRANCE

French recruitment procedures are not excessively formalised, as has increasingly become the case in the UK. Only in the larger companies and state industries is there likely to be a cast-iron recruitment procedure. In some companies personnel matters may be handled with a surprising lack of efficiency.

Recruitment procedures encountered may lead you to believe that the French take a very hit-and-miss view of choosing the people with whom they are to work. In actual fact this is untrue. Employers place more emphasis on personal rapport than technical assessment of a candidate's suitability. That said, paper qualifications are treated with (often undue) reverence too.

Initial applications
The form of the intial application—whether written, by telephone, or personal—will usually be clearly indicated in the job advertisement.

Personal applications are usually only requested for lower-grade jobs and casual employment.

Written applications tend to be more usual than telephoned ones. The trend towards telephoning for an informal discussion on the post, which has become popular in the UK, is by no means widespread. If, however, a telephoned application is requested then a written application would usually prove fruitless, due to the time delay involved.

Where a written application is to be used then the format is exactly the same as in the UK. That is, a two-part package consisting of a letter of application and a CV or curriculum vitae; the French have adopted this name and abbreviation for a biography or career history exactly the same as in the UK.

The importance of rapport

No matter what the format of the initial application, personal meetings and rapport are very important in France. Employers prefer to recruit those whom they feel fit in well, with great regard to personality and attitude, rather than those who merely fit a closely defined profile.

In consequence, it is usually very easy to get an interview. This should not be taken as a good indication of success as can be the case in the UK. Indeed, an initial interview may be merely a weeding out technique, no matter how much time and trouble appears to have been taken in arranging it.

Selection techniques

The use of aptitude tests (le test d'aptitude) and other modern recruitment tools is growing in France but is still surprisingly rare. If used, they are unlikely to be overly demanding in relation to the average level of intelligence of the candidates anticipated to apply; they may even appear childishly simple.

One tool which French recruiters, even in fairly small companies, do treasure is that of **handwriting analysis** using the services of an expert graphologist. This is taken remarkably seriously. If a job advertisement requests your application to be made in your own handwriting this is probably the reason why, though a typewritten application would rarely disqualify you from further selection.

One of the most important selection techniques used in France is, once again, that of personal rapport—and also personal appearance. First impressions really do count and a meeting can be fudged in the first few minutes. Similarly, if you do strike up a good rapport you could well become a prime contender even if your skills, experience and

The French recruitment procedure is often different to the UK one in that selection tests and checks on eligibility are often carried out *before* the interview, not after as is more usual in the UK:

```
┌─────────────────────────────────┐
│     ADVERTISEMENT APPEARS       │
└─────────────────────────────────┘
              │
              ▼
┌─────────────────────────────────┐
│   YOU SUBMIT AN APPLICATION     │
└─────────────────────────────────┘
              │
              ▼
┌─────────────────────────────────┐
│   ATTEND FOR SELECTION TEST     │
└─────────────────────────────────┘
              │
              ▼
┌─────────────────────────────────┐
│      IF SUCCESSFUL, YOUR        │
│    QUALIFICATIONS MAY BE        │
│   EXAMINED AND REFERENCES       │
│          TAKEN UP               │
└─────────────────────────────────┘
              │
              ▼
┌─────────────────────────────────┐
│    ON PASSING THIS STAGE –      │
│     PROCEED TO INTERVIEW        │
└─────────────────────────────────┘
              │
              ▼
┌─────────────────────────────────┐
│     ACCEPTED OR REJECTED        │
└─────────────────────────────────┘
```

Fig 7. The recruitment procedure

Applying for Jobs in France

qualifications are not exactly in line with what the recruiter had in mind.

HOW DO YOU WRITE YOUR APPLICATION?

It is especially important to prepare your letter of application thoroughly and carefully. Generally, the French take anything written in a letter very seriously indeed. It is important that everything written is true, factually correct and provable as such. Claims made in letters are likely to be checked, or stored away and brought out at a later date.

If submitting a letter as a job application do not necessarily expect that it will be replied to by way of a letter. The French have a dislike for writing letters for most other purposes—due to the fact that they commit information to the record!

Anglais ou Français?

A particular problem occurs in the selection of language for letters. Obviously it is a courtesy to write in French, and fairly easy to get a translation done, but this may cause problems later if you do not also *speak* French to that standard. It will be easier to write in English, but the reader may not understand it or may not want to understand it. This is particularly important in France where letters in foreign languages can even go so far as to cause offence.

Generally, the procedure is:

- If you speak *good* French, write in French (even if you need help with the writing).

- If you speak *little* or *no* French, write in English. This may not give a good impression, but you may score points by demonstrating your command of a foreign language.

- If you speak *moderate* French, have a letter translated into French, but keep it fairly simple so as not to over-represent your abilities.

A good compromise if writing in English is to attach a French translation. This will help redeem you in the eyes of the employer!

Translations

It is fairly easy to get good French translations in all parts of the UK. See in your *Yellow Pages* under Translators and Interpreters. At the time of writing the cost should not exceed more than approximately £50 per 1,000 words, even for a complex letter.

If possible, ensure that your translator is familiar with employment correspondence. If you have technical qualifications or experience then you may need a technical translator. Be wary about using willing friends-of-a-friend unless you are satisfied they are competent.

Special advice
Whether you write in French or English it is useful, no matter what your standard of French or English, to have your letter, CV and application forms read over by a native French speaker. If they seem puzzled, or worse still laugh, you will know that something needs changing. Like the worst 'la plume de ma tante' school French even accurate, well translated French can seem too stilted to an employer.

Style and approach
In the UK, a letter of application can be a complex work of art. In France it should essentially be very simple, no matter what your standard of French or the job applied for. In the first instance, this is a courtesy to the reader. However, it is also important because the French are not great letter writers and do not commit more than the essential details to paper.

Letters should be simple and clear. Do not go into excessive detail. Do not elaborate on any point unless absolutely essential. Stick to the facts, with minimal editorial.

The French style of letter is generally quite old-fashioned. The appropriate greetings and closing paragraph are antiquated compared to modern, spoken French but are still in common use.

Above all, people tend to write very cold, uncompromising letters which are rarely, if ever, friendly, chatty or humorous. This should not be taken as rudeness as it is almost certainly not the case. Do not be shocked to receive a curt, formal letter, especially when you have met or talked on the phone to the interviewer or employer and seemed to have established a good rapport.

Things to avoid
Anything which might be misunderstood: colloquialisms or puns (even French ones if you know them), jokes, humour and any abbrevations. French abbreviations are notoriously ambiguous and details of educational qualifications, for example, will need to be quoted in full.

What should you say?
After considering the style of your letter there are certain things which should be included if at all possible. That said, it is important to get them in in as little space as possible—do not ramble on.

For the vast majority of situations there are certain key 'bites' of information that an employer would expect or like to hear. Try to combine these within an overall well presented and well written letter:

- Formally state you are interested in this job (could be achieved by a heading to the letter).

- State where you heard about this vacancy: *France-Soir*?, l'ANPE?

- Provide some information about yourself.

- State your educational qualifications. Explain them if appropriate.

- Provide some information about your experience, with the emphasis on experience rather than career history.

- State your anticipated salary—'votre prétentions'. This may be requested in the advertisement anyway. It is quite common for advertisements *not* to state the salary on offer.

- State your absolute desire for wanting to work in France, and for this company.

- Formal ending, similar to 'Yours faithfully', 'Yours sincerely'. See sample letter in Figure 8.

Special tip
If your ability in French is not extensive then there is a way round this! The solution is to use a standard cover letter (Figure 8) and accompany it with a standard CV. This will provide the information which the employer expects without having to stretch your knowledge of French!

Presentation
Presentation is particularly important for job applications and great care should be taken. As in the UK presentation of the application may be used as an initial weeding-out technique where more applications are received than was anticipated.

Using handwriting
It is perfectly acceptable to hand-write every letter of application. Indeed, employers may prefer this—to facilitate handwriting analysis—and may request this, 'la lettre de candidature manuscrite',

in their advertisement.

If handwriting note that the style of written French is highly cursive and elaborate in presentation: never print anything in a letter! Never omit accents. Note the difference between the figure '1' and '7', '7' and '7'.

Using copies
Generally, every letter should be individually prepared. Carbon copies or photocopies of letters are not suitable (although it is perfectly acceptable to send a photocopied CV).

Layout
Letters should be set out very much as in the UK (see Figure 8). Note the importance of stating the place of writing, as well as the date, together with a heading giving the subject matter in the top right-hand corner, not at the start of the letter.

Materials
A4- or quarto-size paper, always in white, and typed or written in black, is suitable for most purposes. Do not use notepad-size paper.

Addressing the letter
Nine times out of ten your application letter should be addressed to the company or personnel department, rather than a named individual: 'Merci d'adresser votre candidature au Service du Personnel'. Frequently there will also be a reference number to be quoted in the letter too.

Sample letter of application
The sample letter in Figures 8, 9 and 10 will help indicate style, content and presentation. It can be used as it stands as the most simple form of letter to accompany a CV.

HOW DO YOU PREPARE A CV?

Use of the CV
The CV is becoming well established in France as a document most enthusiatic job seekers should have. Certainly, all executive and professional people should have one, together with most people working in commercial fields. Many skilled workers are also now using CVs. The French have adopted the term curriculum vitae and abbreviation CV just as in the UK.

Applying for Jobs in France

>
> John Smith,
> 1 High Street,
> Leeds.
> West Yorkshire.
> LS1 1AA
> Angleterre.
>
> Leeds, le 5 janvier 1993
>
> Référence: Votre annonce dans
> 'les Echos' no 16.180

Service du personnel,
Cambronne Auto,
100 avenue Branly,
75019 Paris.

Messieurs,

En reponse à votre annonce parue ce jour dans 'les Echos', je me permets de poser ma candidature au poste de ....

Veuillez trouvez ci-joint mon curriculum vitae.

Dans l'espoir que vous voudrez bien considérer favorablement ma demande et dans l'attente de votre reponse, je vous prie d'agréer, Messieurs, l'assurance de mes sentiments distingués.

John Smith.

P.J.C.V.

Fig. 8. Sample application letter in French

>John Smith,
>1 High Street,
>Leeds.
>West Yorkshire.
>LS1 1AA
>England.

>5 January 1993

Personnel Department,
Cambronne Auto,
100 Avenue Branly,
75019 Paris.

Dear Sirs,

Your Advertisement in 'The Times', 5 January 1993.

In reply to your advertisement in today's 'The Times' I wish to apply for the post of ....
....

Please find enclosed my C.V.

I hope the enclosed will be of interest and I look forward to hearing from you.

Yours faithfully,

John Smith.

Encl. C.V.

Fig. 9. Sample application letter in English.

HOW TO ADDRESS YOUR ENVELOPE CORRECTLY

```
Monsieur LECLERC,
Chef du Personnel,
CAMBRONNE AUTO,
100 avenue Branly,
75019 PARIS,
FRANCE,
```

Fig. 10. How to address your envelope correctly. Note the use of capital letters for the surname, company name, town or city and country—but not for 'avenue' or 'rue' etc. Do not state the region or département as this is indicated by the postal code which appears BEFORE the town name.

Pointers on compiling a CV

Length and detail
French CVs should be as short as possible, whilst incorporating the necessary information. Never elaborate or provide undue detail. Information should be accurate and provable; as with letters it is liable to be checked.

Type
CVs should usually be set out chronologically when listing both education and career history.

Emphasis
If anything, French CVs should focus on educational achievements, both at school and university, and any subsequent vocational qualifications and training certificates. If possible it can help to state what the French equivalent of your UK qualification is, even if it is one that is not yet officially recognised as equal.

Other information
Do not present more than the most basic information about hobbies

CURRICULUM VITAE

Nom, Prénom:	SMITH, Jane
Adresse:	1 The Road, York, North Yorkshire YO1 1AA, Angleterre.
Téléphone:	Domicile – (19 44 000) 456789 Bureau – (19 44 000) 456789
Lieu de Naissance:	York, Angleterre
Date de Naissance:	1.1.65
Nationalité:	Britannique
Situation de Famille:	Célibataire
Langues:	Anglais (langue maternelle) Français (parlé et écrit couramment)

Formation:

1981-1983	A levels (diplôme de fin d'études secondaires, équivalent du baccalauréat) en économie, français, géographie.
1983-1986	BSc (licence) en géographie. Université de York.

Expérience Professionnelle:

1986-1987	Vendeuse stagiaire, A&B Black Limited, Londres.
1987-1988	Vendeuse, A& B Black Limited, Londres.
depuis 1989	Directeur du service d'exportations, Uvichem Limited, Reading.

Autres Renseignements:
Permis de conduire.
Je lis l'espagnol.
Prête à travailler à l'étranger.

Fig. 11. Sample French CV.

and interests, unless they are highly relevant to your work. The French are not too concerned about your out-of-hours activities and long descriptions of your interest in birdwatching or photography may come across as extremely curious.

Referees
Usually, the addresses of referees are not included in the CV. If asked for they can be given on a separate sheet.

Photographs
It is becoming common but by no means customary to attach a recent photograph to your CV. Be sure to do this if it is requested in the job advertisement: 'Merci d'adresser lettre, CV et photo'. Otherwise you can choose to do so if you think it would help; doing so when it has not been requested will never look odd.

Presenting the CV

There is very little variation in the presentation of a French CV. The appropriate order is indicated on the sample in Figure 11. The CV should always be typed and, preferably, on one sheet of paper only. Photocopied CVs are quite acceptable, although professional and executive people are now starting to have their CVs laser-printed.

As with letters take care to use accents correctly. Also note that when quoting figures a period, not a comma or space, is used in French between the hundreds and thousands, and a comma instead of a decimal point. Eg: 100,000.00 in French writing is 100.000,00. Explain obscure abbreviations.

With care it is possible to present your CV in a way that the necessary information is obvious, no matter what the language of the reader.

Sample CV

The sample in Figure 11 will show what to include in your French CV and how to present it. It can be used as it stands simply by replacing with your own details or lifting the information from your own CV.

HANDLING APPLICATION FORMS

The use of application forms is not quite as extensive in France as the UK. For senior, middle-management and many commercial jobs the CV has largely replaced it. At the lower end of the jobs market many employers rely on a brief personal interview, rather than spend time creating further paperwork.

Having said this you may well encounter an application form. In some situations this may be supplied to be filled in *after* your letter of

Name:	Nom
Address:	Adresse
Telephone:	Téléphone
Date of birth:	Date de naissance
Place of birth:	Lieu de naissance
Nationality:	Nationalité
Education:	Études/Formation
Work experience:	Expérience professionelle
Reference:	Référence
Interests outside work:	Activités extra-professionnelles
Other information:	Autre renseignements
Date:	Date

Figure 12. How to decode the application form.

application, or even after an interview. This document will then form part of your personnel records and it therefore needs to be treated as such.

Filling in forms

Application forms are rarely that onerous to complete. Any good French dictionary can be used to decipher the vast majority of questions. In many cases it is possible to give one-word answers which do not strain your skills in written French and, of course, answers such as name and address and qualifications are the same in any language.

A good technique is to photocopy the application form and then complete a rough version first, before proceeding to the original. If you are able to have a native French speaker proofread the form for you then so much the better.

Special tip

If presented with an application form which you do not understand, one technique is to dispense with it entirely and, instead, submit your CV, even where this has not been requested. Although this may not find favour with the employer it is preferable to submitting a badly completed form.

The dossier

For some jobs in France, primarily executive ones, a simple letter or

CV is insufficient. In these cases you may be asked for a portfolio of career information: a 'dossier de candidature'. In most cases this should comprise:

- a letter of application, handwritten, with indication of salary required;
- a current CV;
- a current photograph;
- testimonials from previous employers (if available);
- academic certificates (copies are acceptable but they should be certified).

INTERVIEWS

Interviews are very important to the average French employer. They provide an opportunity for personal contact, which is regarded as all-important. Jobs are often lost and won on the basis of personal rapport, so an interview can be more demanding than might otherwise be expected.

Interview styles

The formal interview is still more common in France than the UK. The 'cosy chat over coffee' is not as popular as it now is in the UK, although there is a movement towards it, especially in the south of France in modern, sunrise industries. A telephone call to the secretary in the personnel department can often reveal whether you will face a formal or informal interview, a chat or a grilling!

Rapport
French bosses place great importance on getting to know the whole person. Most consider themselves shrewd judges of character. The only quality that can rank in importance with the ability to conduct a good interview is the right piece of paper from the right school or university.

Language ability
The importance of French
There can only be one recommendation when attending an interview in France. That is, you will score an innumerable number of merit points if you speak good French. It is only in the last two or three years that the ability to speak foreign languages (like English) has become a major selling point for the foreign employee.

If you have stated a certain knowledge of French in your application then you can expect it will be tested. If your ability really is minimal then it is best to admit this and aim to secure positions where this will not be a problem (see below).

What about the employer?
Contrary to popular belief the French are often no better linguistically than the British. But they do like to see their language used by foreigners—and correctly, too. Some will even be offended or annoyed if you cannot speak French or speak it badly. They may even reject the application or finish the interview in extreme cases.

When may French not be necessary?
There are two main exceptions to the need to speak French at interview and, indeed, for a job in France:

- Professional, scientific, technical staff, etc: If you have sound experience in a specialist field your ability in French may be unimportant. It also applies where the employer is having to recruit a foreigner because such skills are not available locally.

- Where English language ability is part of the job: There are some jobs in France where having an employee who speaks English as a mother tongue is a major coup for the employer. For example, secretarial work, teaching, jobs with tourists. Also, look for advertisements which state 'vous êtes parfaitement bilingue anglais': literally, 'you are bilingual in English'.

Special tip
In cases where you do not expect to speak French at interview, check if an interpreter will be provided. Alternatively, it may be preferable for you to hire an interpreter who is sympathetic to you, rather than one of the interviewer's choice.

What to take

Documents and items which may be required at interview should be prepared in advance. Many of them are easier to prepare and obtain in the UK, rather than once abroad. Some documents, although not required for interview, may be needed for contractual and residence permit regulations if the job is offered.

Documents and certificates can also act as a talking point—or even a diversion—if the interview drifts to subjects which you find difficult to discuss in French.

Suggested documents to take:

- Copies of application letter and form for reference.
- Copies of CV for reference and distribution.
- Supply of photographs.
- References. Could have translated into French.
- Academic certificates. Employers will not usually take your word for it. If you take copies they should be certified (stamped and signed) by the issuing authority.
- Birth and marriage certificates.
- Specimens of your work, if appropriate, eg designs.
- Documented case histories of projects completed for past employees (if not confidential).

Etiquette and presentation

Correct etiquette and presentation at an interview are regarded as extremely important in France. Even in cases where the interview might seem a fairly informal occasion—maybe even at a café—it should not be treated as such. The interviewer is sure to be taking the whole matter very seriously.

Dress and appearance
Dress and appearance are very important to the French. They should be smart and contemporary. Certainly for most commercial positions men should wear a dark, sombre suit with shirt and tie. Women should wear a simple but elegant dress; ideally never trousers. Fashionability and quality are very important; certainly so far as executive positions go quality labels and high price tags will win friends and influence people.

First impressions
You are unlikely to give an unfavourable impression by following rather old-fashioned rules of etiquette. Be sure to shake hands (but do not kiss!). Sit only when asked. Do not smoke unless the interviewer does (but hardly any French companies have no-smoking policies). Addressing the interview as Monsieur or Madame is usually most appropriate.

How should you deal with the interviewer?

Making allowances
Generally, the interviewer won't make a lot of allowances for the fact that French is not your first language, or that you are foreign. In certain situations he or she may cherish the fact! It is quite in order to ask for clarification of a question you do not understand. However, if you can conduct the interview as coherently as possible you will gain

added kudos.

The inquisition
Expect a very direct and searching line of questioning. Sometimes the questions may seem rude, but they are just the French way of gaining a positive answer unfettered by the need to be polite. Be especially prepared for questions for which there is no right or wrong answer.
Be prepared to give short answers. French bosses can quickly become impatient. But do take care not to give ambiguous, incorrect or untrue answers. Your responses are likely to be recorded and more searching questions asked later on. Shallow answers are likely to be spotted immediately; always be ready for 'Puis-je vous demander de clarifier?' (could you clarify/explain it please?).

Poacher turned gamekeeper
Interviewers are likely to want to make you sweat and petition them for a job, but try not to become too desperate. A typical French technique is also to reverse the line of questioning. After persistently asking you to give reason after reason why you should be appointed, the interviewer switches tack and demands to know why someone apparently so well qualified is not seeking a position with a larger/longer established/more successful company!

What questions may be asked?
It may be useful to consider what answers you would offer to the following questions, as experience has shown that they crop up in a surprising number of interviews:

- Why do you want to work in France?

- Why do you want to work for this company?

- What differences do you envisage between working in France and working in the UK?

- What do you think you can contribute from your knowledge of foreign (British) work practices/technology/procedure etc?

- What gaps exist in your training? (It does not matter so much if there are gaps between your training and that of your potential French colleagues so long as you are aware of them.)

- Do you plan to live in France permanently? (Conceivably a trick question if the job advertisement has stated travel is involved.)

- What do your family think?

- Where do you expect yourself and this company to be in five years? In ten years?

Ice-breakers and fill-ins
Before the interview make sure you know a little about the company to which you are applying. This will enable you to make an informed and intelligent response to 'Y a-t-il des questions?' (Are there any questions?) which is sure to come sooner or later!

It is also very helpful to have some knowledge of French culture, history, geography, food and wine—force yourself to learn if you are not really interested. All these can be used as ice-breakers at the start and finish of an interview and will invariably flatter. Avoid the weather (not done in France as in most countries outside the UK!).

Points worth making

It is important not to let the interviewer have all their own way, although it can be very difficult to get a chance to make the points that you feel are important. Avoid taking over, which can cause great annoyance. However, interviewers tend to respect those who introduce purposeful points which add something to the interview.

The following points and matters are worth making or stressing, assuming they have not already been covered by the interviewer's line of questioning:

- Stress the value of your academic qualifications. Explain what they mean or involve and, if they are considered prestigious in the UK, make that clear. Stress the reputation of any schools, colleges or universities attended.

- Explain the value of your work experience, if possible with reference to projects you have worked on. If your past employers are notable in the UK for particular achievements point this out.

- Family background. Would rarely be drawn upon in the UK but worth mentioning in France if your particular trade or profession runs in the family.

- Examples of successful projects you have worked on (with documentary evidence to support if possible).

- Show a knowledge and acceptance of problems you will experience in adapting to France, and suggestions as to how you will tackle them.

- Exhibit knowledge of this company. If possible, refer to specific projects they have worked on. Make suggestions for business development or improvements (tactfully).

- Be prepared to talk money and conditions of service. The French are not as reticent to discuss this as in the UK.

- Finally, affirm your level of interest. State that you are looking forward to being considered. Say that you hope to make the next stage of selection. Never leave the interviewer to assume that because you are here you are interested. The French interviewer likes to be courted!

CHECKLIST OF KEY POINTS

1. Check your qualifications. Are they acceptable in France? Action needed to enable this? What are the French equivalents?

2. How closely do you meet the requirements the employer will expect? Can you change the way you work, or not?

3. Draft copy for letters of application, CV and forms beforehand. Do they all stand up to scrutiny?

4. Review your interview technique. What will you do differently from an interview in the UK?

4
Working in France

RESIDENCE IN FRANCE

What are your rights?
- Citizens of one EC country, such as the UK, have a right to live and work in France under EC regulations. The same right applies to all other EC countries.
- No work permit is necessary.
- No visa is necessary.
- No visa is necessary to go to France to look for a job.
- All that is required to live in France and work there is a **residence permit**. This is obtainable once you move to France. You do not need one, nor any other special permission, *before* moving to France. The residence permit must be obtained within three months of arrival.

(NB. Permits are required for Monaco. Consult the French Consulate.)

Obtaining a permit
To get a residence permit, which is known as a Carte de Séjour, you should apply to the nearest appropriate authority once you are in France. They will supply the necessary forms. Apply at either the préfecture in large towns or the mairie, which is the town hall, in a smaller town or village. Any local person will usually be able to direct you there.

Possible problems
Some préfecture and mairie officials are very unhelpful and at least claim to know nothing of the procedure to be followed. Others are said to be very helpful. Also, the procedure to be followed, and the documents to be produced, vary somewhat from office to office. Different officials interpret the rules differently. Therefore, do prepare well beforehand as regards the documents you may need.

What documents do I need?
Your application must be accompanied by:

- A valid 10-year passport.
- Three passport photographs.
- Your birth certificate.
- Marriage certificate (if applicable). Birth and marriage certificates should be translated into French by an authorised translator. It is easier to get this done before leaving for France; your local French Consulate will supply a list of approved translators.
- Proof of accommodation. This may be required. A receipt for rent or proof of property purchase will suffice (ask the notaire who handled your house purchase).
- Proof of employment. You will need to produce a contract of employment; some places will accept a letter from the employer instead.

What if I do not have a job?
If you do not have a job, ie you are staying in France to look for work, you may only stay for three months. No Carte de Séjour is needed for this period. If at the end of three months you have not found work it is possible to be granted an extension of stay by applying to the préfecture or mairie. (Experience tells that this is rarely granted.) Most people in this situation would merely travel back to the UK for a while before re-entering France on another three-month, permit-free stay.

Be prepared
Some Carte de Séjour applicants have been asked for medical certificates, proof of no criminal record, dates of birth and places of birth of both your parents and also grandparents. Many legal and official processes in France require this information and all French nationals have documentation to prove all these particulars.

Carry the Carte!
Eventually you will be granted a Carte de Séjour which should now last for an indefinite period (older ones are renewable). This should be carried at all times and produced to the police on request. If you have a family your dependants are entitled to residence also, if you have been granted it.

EMPLOYMENT LAW AND CONTRACTS OF EMPLOYMENT

The system of employment law which exists in all the EC countries is that which has been developed in each individual country. This applies to France as well. However, there will be some changes as a result of forthcoming EC laws.

The future
The EC is committed to harmonising (that is, making identical or similar) terms and conditions of employment throughout all the EC. In effect, this will mean that hours of work and holiday entitlements will be the same in all EC countries—all further policies to develop the Single Market within Europe. At present, however, the systems in each individual country still apply. At the time of writing it is not known exactly when harmonisation will be achieved.

The present
Currently, employment law in France is wholly French law. This is more complex than UK employment law and many regulations apply which are unknown in the UK (such as minimum pay). By and large French employees enjoy better protection but the various entitlements of employees in law do sometimes discourage employers from hiring staff.

Your contract of employment

Coverage
The same employment laws apply to every person working in France, whether French or foreign. If working for a foreign company but based in France your terms of employment will be covered by the law of the appropriate county only if specifically stated in your contract. Otherwise, French law will automatically over-rule any clauses of the contract with which it is at variance.

Verbal contracts
A French contract of employment can be written or verbal. There is no automatic right to have a contract in writing. Although all reputable employers should agree to a request for a written contract, some small businesses may be unprepared for this or unwilling to do so.

Written contracts
You will usually need a written contract of employment, a **Contrat de Travail**, in order to obtain your Carte de Séjour. A contract with an employee, rather than a union, etc, is also known as a **Contrat Individuel**. Contracts will always be supplied in French; never expect one in any other language.

Anything put in writing is always taken very seriously in France.

```
MAGASINS A LECLERC

110 avenue Branly
75019 PARIS

1 00 00 00 00
_____

Service du Personnel

                    CONTRAT INDIVIDUEL

(Etabli en application du décret numéro 11-123 du 31 avril 1993
relatif à la situation.)

Entre :

MAGASINS A LECLERC, 110 avenue Branly, 75019 PARIS

et le contratant soussigné :

1ére : Mr, précédement en fonction auprès l'établissement
MAGASINS A LECLERC, 110 avenue Branly, 75019 PARIS occupera les
fonctions de COMPTABLE du 1 juin 1993 auprès du même
établissement, MAGASINS A LECLERC, 110 avenue Branly, 75019
PARIS.

2e : Le contratant reconnaît avoir pris connaisance de la
lettre de mission annexe à cet contrat et qui en fait partie
intégrant.

3e : Pour le calcul de la rémunération et des avantages
accessoires prévus par le décret susvisé notamment en ce qui
concerne les majorations familiales ainsi que pour le régime
des deplacements prévus par les dispositions du décret susvisé
il sera compte de la situation de l'agent qu'elle est fixée ci
dessous :

Nom, Prénom              : SMITH, John
Adresse                  : 76500 ROUEN
Grade                    : COMPTABLE
Situation de famille     : CELIBATAIRE
Numéro sécurité sociale  : 1234561234561

(Changement ultérieur de cette situation dûment notifié
entraînera de droit à sa date d'effet les changements résultant
de l'application des décrets précités.)
```

Fig 13. Specimen contract of employment.

Therefore, it is important to have the contract translated, or at the very least have someone you can trust explain the main provisions to you. In the case of many skilled or unskilled workers the terms of the contract will have been negotiated and agreed by the appropriate trade union. As long as there are no alterations to the form you can be quietly confident that the terms are acceptable. Executives and professional people may find that an individual contract is prepared for them and this may require further study to avoid the inclusion of any unfavourable clauses.

What conditions to expect in your contract

Very important: As there is no necessity to issue a written Contrat de Travail there is no legal basis for what topics must be covered in that contract. The clauses which can be incorporated are purely a matter between yourself and the employer.

No contract of employment can overturn French law. For example, the French constitution confers the right to strike and so a no-strike deal in a contract cannot be enforced.

Standard forms

There is no standard form Contrat de Travail in use in France. Most companies prepare their own and this will vary from employer to employer. If you do not wish to use the employer's contract, or they do not have one, you may write your own.

Although French contracts can be very long and complex they are frequently very short, stating only:

- name and address of both parties
- job title
- place of work
- pay scale coefficient and how negotiated.

Having said all this, it would be prudent to ensure that the following terms are included in your contract:

- job title and description of duties;
- rate of pay, not just what scale applies;
- bonuses, benefits and commissions;
- hours of work; holiday entitlement;
- outline of responsibilities;
- who is your immediate superior;
- status or grade in company hierarchy;
- procedure in case of disputes;
- notice required by either party;

- severance terms, in case of redundancy;
- disciplinary and dismissal procedure.

Check

It is common for contracts of employment to refer to the terms contained in the offer of employment letter when the offer of the job is made. If so, it is prudent to insist that the offer letter is attached as an appendix to the contract. Contracts are valid on acceptance: they do not necessarily have to be signed.

Basic principles of employment law

French law sets down a large number of rules and regulations by which both employers and employees must abide. These are generally more expansive than in the UK. Whether or not a contract of employment refers to any or all of these laws is largely immaterial. It is taken as read that these rules apply. They cannot be circumvented by clauses in a contract.

Collective agreements

The system of collective agreements (**Conventions Collectives**) is central to employment law in France and refers to a situation whereby employees' bodies and employers' organisations must come together to negotiate terms of service. More information on this system is given later.

The law is a minimum

Employment law in France is deceptive. The regulations that apply only set down a minimum standard. It is very common for employers to exceed the minimum standard as a recruitment incentive. If you accept a job on minimum legal standards it is likely that you will be getting a poor deal. The effect of this system is that it gives the employer power—to grant or withdraw benefits as an incentive—but still remain within the law.

Is the law respected?

The situation as regards application of the law is fairly uniform. Most employers still stick to the rules. A very few smaller ones do not, but deviations are usually subject to the consent of both parties. This is often because the work is carried out for cash, no questions asked!

Currently the situation is liable to change—not only are EC reforms due but, in any case, the French Government is committed to simplifying employment legislation and making it easier for employers to employ people. For example, it is no longer necessary for employers to obtain official permission to make redundancies, as it once used to be.

The main provisions of French employment law are as follows.

Minimum wages (the SMIC)
France has minimum wage legislation under which a minimum hourly rate is fixed by the Government. This is known as the **SMIC (Salaire Minimum Interprofessionnel de Croissance)**.
Further details are given in the section on rates of pay, page 84.

Working hours
The statutory working week is 39 hours. Up to 44 hours per week is allowed as long as the average over a year does not exceed 39 hours. Most French companies start at 8.30am and finish at 4.30 or 5pm.

Those under 18 (and women, in some circumstances) may not be required to work at night.

The working week for shift workers, where an operation works around the clock, is limited to 35 hours.

Flexitime (horaire flexible) operates in some companies.

Overtime
Overtime (heures supplementaires) in excess of the arrangement above must be officially approved. It must be paid at the rate of 125 per cent of the usual rate for the first six hours and then 150 per cent for the rest of the overtime worked.

Holiday entitlement
The minimum holiday entitlement is five weeks paid leave plus 11 public holidays. However, some companies offer more as a recruitment inducement so the actual situation should be checked.

Often summer holidays may not be taken at any time; a month-long close down of a company in July or August is still common.

Period of notice
The statutory period of notice is typically one month, from either the employer or the employee, but this can vary (usually to the advantage of the employee).

Redundancy
Companies are now permitted to make staff redundant for economic reasons without obtaining official permission, as used to be the case.

Employees are entitled to redundancy payment related to the length of service. Details of this can be obtained from the relevant collective agreement which governs the job. Many companies offer more than the statutory minimum.

If you are made redundant you may seek advice from the local **l'Inspection du Travail**, and may refer the matter to an industrial tribunal at which the employer will have to justify the redundancy.

Training (Formation)

Each company in France is obliged by law to consider the training and on-going career development requirements of their employees. This is achieved by the compulsory allocation of 1.2 per cent of the gross payroll amount towards training.

Training can be provided in two ways. A company can either organise its own in-house training programmes, or pay specialist training companies to provide this. Every employer is entitled to apply to take a statutory amount of paid leave (called **CIF**) to further his or her work skills and vocational qualifications.

In addition, **GRETA** organisations provide training courses at weekends to study for vocational qualifications, and which in this case the employee may choose to attend.

Details can be obtained from the personnel department of the company concerned and also in many cases from the works council.

Dismissal

It is extremely difficult to dismiss staff unless under the terms of a formal redundancy plan. Generally, staff may only be dismissed without redundancy payments becoming necessary in cases of:

1. Negligence.
2. Professional misconduct.

If dismissed, advice can be sought from the l'Inspection du Travail.

Disciplinary procedures

The disciplinary procedures which apply in most companies are very similar and governed by the appropriate collective agreement. In cases of negligence or professional misconduct the member of staff can usually be dismissed without warning. However, most companies subscribe to the following system:

- First offence: Verbal reprimand.
- Second offence: Formal written warning.
- Third offence: A period of suspension, without pay, can be given to the employee. The length of this is determined by the employer.
- Fourth offence: Immediate dismissal without warning.

Those who become subject to the disciplinary procedure should seek advice from their shop steward or works council immediately.

What about part-time workers?
Part-time workers are entitled to exactly the same rights and benefits as full-time workers. They should receive the same salary as someone undertaking the same job full-time, but on a pro-rata basis.

What about public employees?
Employees working for government departments, local authorities and nationalised industries have the same rights as those in the private sector. Public employees also have a special status in which their jobs are effectively guaranteed for life.

WHAT SHOULD YOU DO ABOUT DISPUTES AT WORK?

In the past the relationship between French employers and employees was very confrontational; both parties rarely came together in serious negotiations and strikes were common. In recent years a more conciliatory situation has emerged. Employment law now encourages both parties to come together and negotiate, even before disputes arise—thus the collective agreements.

Clear channels for settling disputes exist in most companies, and great importance is placed on using the official channels at the earliest stage. These channels are accessible to foreign workers at all levels.

In France a problem or dispute at work is regarded as either:

- collective; that is, it affects the whole work force or a significant group;
- or individual, in that it affects one employee only.

In either case the procedure for reaching settlement is the same:

1. Contact your immediate superior and advise them of the problem or dispute.

2. If no solution is found: Contact your shop steward or works council representative (**délégué syndical**, or **délégué du personnel** in larger companies). They will decide if the dispute is individual or collective and make representations to the management. At this stage the matter is dealt with internally.

3. The Direction Départementale du Travail et de l'Emploi or l'Inspection du Travail (see telephone directory) can provide further advice and information.

4. If no solution is found: The matter is usually referred to your trade union or professional association for advice. It is usually only at this stage that an individual dispute can become a collective one, to be dealt with at regional or even national level.

5. Finally, if no solution can be found: The problem can be referred to an **industrial tribunal** (the **Conseil des Prud'hommes**). The matter can be pursued by the individual but it is preferable to have the support of your union or professional association.

RATES OF PAY AND OTHER BENEFITS

General levels

Rates of pay in France compare very favourably with both those in the UK and Europe as a whole. They are typically *higher* than the UK though not as high as those in, for example, Germany. Most people moving from the UK would expect to earn more in France, assuming that they were employed in an equivalent job.

Greater differentials
One important point to realise is that there is a greater differential between unskilled or semi-skilled workers and executives or professional people than in the UK. In France a secretary might earn 30 per cent more than their UK colleague, whereas the managing director of the company could earn almost 100 per cent more than his or her UK counterpart.

Collective agreements (see page 93) apply to the wages paid to most manual and clerical jobs, and many professional jobs too which set minimum agreed pay for specific grades. Only in the more senior posts is the rate individually negotiable. Hence there is great importance attached to status and grade. Having said this, not all companies pay the same rate, as most pay a variable fraction over the agreed minimum as a recruitment incentive.

Many people from countries with lower average wages, such as the UK, find that they are attractive as employees because they are prepared to take lower wages than their French counterparts (although this still represents an increase over their UK wages).

Wages and salaries

In France there is precious little difference between what, in the UK, we would consider wage- or salary-paid staff. Anyone who is working under a full-time contract of employment, even those paid hourly, are considered salaried employees. Most employees are now paid monthly; the traditional way of paying wages in France was two-weekly.

The following examples of salaries have been extracted from the UK press and French press at time of writing. They give some idea of how salaries in each country vary.

	UK	France (equivalent in £)
Junior secretary	£8,250	£10,750
Assistant manager (retail outlet)	£12,000	£15,800
Account executive (advertising industry)	£18,500	£25,345
Engineer (water treatment)	£24,650	£35,040
Director (small company)	£40,000	£68,000

Fig 14. Examples of salaries.

Method of payment
Wages are usually paid at the end of the month by cheque or direct transfer to the employee's bank account. Wages over FF120,000 must be paid in this way and, in any case, there is no entitlement to be paid in cash. Every employee is entitled to a **pay slip (bulletin de paie)** itemising their pay, any deductions made and for what reason.

An important difference
When reading recruitment advertising and negotiating rates of pay it is important to note that wages are usually quoted as gross monthly figures in France, not annually as in the UK; FF12,000 is FF12,000 per month, not annually! If a **13th-** or **14th-month bonus** is given this is extra. In that case the annual salary would be fourteen times the figure quoted.

Minimum wages
As discussed in the previous section France has comprehensive minimum wage legislation. The minimum wage rate is known as the SMIC (Salaire Minimum Interprofessionnel de Croissance) and it is set annually at 2 per cent above the cost of living.

The statement 'SMIC' in a job advertisement affirms that this rate will be offered, although most workers do expect more. 'SMIC + 5 per cent' or 'SMIC + 10 per cent' indicate that the appropriate premium is being offered.

Bonuses and profit sharing

It is becoming increasingly the case that the salary figure quoted for a job does not represent the actual financial package that is being offered. More and more employers are offering **extra payments** to enhance the basic salary. They are above both the minimum set by law (SMIC) and the minimum negotiated in the appropriate collective agreement.

However you should check carefully. The reason for operating a bonus system is not as generous as it might seem. Quite simply, the statutory rates are often quite low in comparison to the actual rate paid including bonuses, which gives the employer power to operate an **incentive system** or link pay to productivity. Most companies that do not already have a bonus scheme are considering them.

Thirteenth-month bonus
Although not compulsory it has become customary to pay staff a thirteenth-month bonus (**treizième mois**), which is an extra month's pay, usually given at Christmas. Some pay a fourteenth-month bonus (**quatorzième mois**) prior to the summer holiday; particulary prevalent in Paris. Alternatively, the thirteenth- and fourteenth-month bonus may be viewed as merely a different way of distributing the salary payments.

Productivity bonus
In addition to thirteenth- and fourteenth-month bonuses, check what **productivity bonuses (primes)** may be available for meeting set targets. These may be collective (that is, they apply to all employees) or individual (negotiated with individual employees only). They typically range between 10–20 per cent; some sales and marketing staff, for example, would expect to add to their salary by up to 20 per cent.

Profit sharing schemes
Many companies in France have now introduced, or are considering, the introduction of a **profit sharing scheme** (a **système d'intéressement aux bénéfices**), and it is worth checking to see what is available. This usually comprises a salary made up of a guaranteed minimum amount plus a further payment linked to the profits (or losses) of the company.

Employers are being encouraged to introduce profit sharing through favourable tax treatment.

Other benefits

French employers and employees are now placing increasing importance on **fringe benefits**. This is principally for tax reasons and also due to the fact that private schemes to top up the basic state social security benefits have become increasingly sought after. Benefits differ somewhat from those in the UK:

- Company cars: These are usually only offered to essential users rather than as a perk. Vehicles (mostly French) tend to be functional rather than prestigious. Casual user car allowances are often payable instead, for employees to use their own car on occasional company business.

- Health insurance: Private health insurance schemes are becoming very common. (With some exceptions the state health insurance scheme does not cover all costs.)

- Social Security: Extra benefits, especially non-contributory pension schemes (**Régime de Retraite Sans Retenues**) are increasingly sought after, although not so much as in the UK, as French state pensions are comparatively generous.

- Housing benefits: These are offered most usually in expensive areas, or to attract personnel to industries in more remote areas. They might include a subsidised mortgage or rent contribution.

- Training: Paid leave for paid training, including paid secondments and sabbaticals, are much more common than in the UK.

Those undertaking a posting to France may qualify for relocation expenses, school fees paid and salaries at the highest international levels—but they must all be negotiated and are not necessarily offered as a matter of course.

WHAT ARE WORKING CONDITIONS LIKE?

In the past, up until the late 1970s, working conditions in France were poor—conceivably some of the poorest in Europe. However, things have changed in recent years and standards in the workplace, and the attitude of the employer to his staff, can now be expected to be at least in line with those in the UK, though often behind Germany and the Scandinavian countries. The French employer is still apt to regard his staff merely as one of the factors of production.

Much depends on the size and status of the company concerned. Large organisations and multinational companies meet all legal standards, and frequently exceed them. In the last two or three years a majority of medium-sized companies in France have recognised the importance of looking after their workforce.

Health and safety
Health and safety legislation is comprehensive. The responsibility for implementing the appropriate regulations is the remit of various government departments, and the works councils who are empowered to monitor and make representations to management concerning health and safety.

How to deal with problems
Some small businesses, especially family businesses, may fail to meet the statutory standards in areas such as health and safety, welfare facilities, training and employee rights. Most, however, subscribe to the minimum rates of pay.

In cases where standards in the workplace fall short the works council should be consulted initially. If this fails the local l'Inspection du Travail or, in severe cases, the Conseil des Prud'hommes (industrial tribunal) can be consulted.

Getting along with colleagues
Integrating into the French working environment may take some adjusting to. Quite apart from the overall cultural differences there are dissimilarities in working practices and attitudes at work. The French have resisted foreign business styles—such as some of the American ideas adopted in UK business—more than any other country in Europe.

Initially the French can be averse to foreigners and can even be or seem hostile. Underneath they usually turn out to be friendly and helpful, but usually only accept foreigners on their terms, not yours. French people are not all that interested in foreigners or different ways of doing things. Even those that initially express some interest may quickly lose interest as the novelty wears off. You may need to work hard at building up a good working relationship for the first 12 months at the very least.

Some possible problems you might encounter amongst your colleagues:

- Outright xenophobia. (Most foreign workers in France are poor African immigrants who are not held in high esteem.)
- Jealousy of your skills and experience.
- Embarrassment that it has been necessary to recruit a foreigner.
- Annoyance at your taking a French job.
- Annoyance at your lack of understanding of France.
- Total unwillingness to accept that you can contribute anything of value.

- Genuinely finding your ways of doing things illogical, even if they are a major improvement over French methods.

Some solutions for dealing with these problems might be:

- Speak good French; praise the French language.
- Get to know about French culture and geography.
- Show a long-term commitment to France (permanent movers are accepted better than posted personnel).
- Introduce changes gradually.
- Ask for your colleagues' opinions even if you are totally convinced that your own methods are best.
- Explain why you are doing things differently, and produce evidence to show the benefits.
- Give orders and instructions with extra tact.

However, be sure to hold your own and stand up for your own country and culture in the workplace. French people are patriotic and whilst admiring foreigners who praise France expect them to show patriotism to their own country too.

What names should you use?
Most people are formal at work. Call them Monsieur or Madame (by itself) initially; Mademoiselle is only for young women. Let *them* decide if first names can be used, which may not always happen. Be particularly careful to use 'vous' rather than 'tu'; the latter can still be taken as an insult if used wrongly, especially with subordinates.

Social situations
Generally, inviting colleagues to social situations is not an easy way to break the ice. Let them take the lead. In the first instance, and when you are sure people are starting to become more familiar, a drink in a bar or café, or visit to a restaurant, would be appropriate.

Do not invite colleagues home until you know then quite well but, done properly, this will be considered a great honour. Do not be surprised if colleagues do not invite you to their home for some considerable time; the French are sometimes unduly ashamed of their homes and they may prefer to run up a large restaurant bill to entertain you instead.

What will the boss expect?
Generally, French bosses are very demanding and will expect high standards; this will certainly be commensurate with the salary you are

being paid if you have negotiated a favourable package. If you have promised any particular results then you can be sure results will be expected. If you have committed them to paper then this will be taken very seriously indeed!

Handling negative attitudes
French employers, though now recognising the need to recruit foreigners, can have a very negative attitude once you are in the workplace. They may doubt that you will be able to fit into the French way, nor bring any tangible benefits to the company. Although you may have been hired for your knowledge of foreign methods they may worry that you will shatter the cosy French status quo which exists, especially in long established companies.

Some solutions to the problems which may be created are:

- avoid making rash promises;
- set only realistic targets and make sure they are achieved;
- keep a record of your success as proof;
- do not dismiss French ideas without good reason;
- do not introduce foreign ideas wholesale;
- push your personal advantages, eg native English-speaking;
- always keep superiors informed of your progress.

The hierarchy

The hierarchy of staff is one of the *most* important influences in the French workplace. Quite simply, in any given company there will be a hierarchy of superiority and inferiority, denoted either by job title, salary, or even length of service.

Make attempts to find out about the hierarchy, though much is down to unwritten rules. Many bridges can be built by observing it, and many doors snapped shut by riding roughshod over the system. For example, approaches to a supplier or customer company should always be made to your counterpart in that company; to go higher or lower is to undermine someone's authority, or rob them of their status.

The cadre
The cadre system is totally unknown in the UK but crucial in French business. The cadre are senior executives who have received a certain education (often Grandes Ecoles) and have particular, prestigious qualifications. They have accrued certain experience, often with the 'right companies' or government departments.

A cadre is usually a very competent and well paid individual. However, critics of this elitist system say that a cadre has only achieved this through having the right education and right contacts, usually through family connections, regardless of ability.

It is almost impossible for those without the right background to achieve cadre status and hence the most prestigous jobs. For example, an 'ingenieur' and a 'technicien' are principally both engineers but the 'ingenieur' is a cadre; the 'technicien' can rarely attain his or her superior's pay and status no matter how competent he or she may be.

Foreign employees aspiring to cadre-type status may manage to evade this career bar by emphasising their education and contacts, and in emphasising their foreign origin, staying aloof from the system.

Promotion and prospects
Promotion in France is typically according to 'l'ancienneté' (long service) rather than merit; many able people have been left standing waiting for dead men's shoes! Only in the last few years have employers started to circumvent the hierarchy and pick out and promote those who show promise.

The best policy for avoiding this problem is to ensure that your achievements are both recognised and recorded. Failing this, a move to a more progressive employer may be the only solution.

TRADES UNIONS AND WORKS COUNCILS

Trades unions

Trades unions (**syndicats**) are well established in France and there is a right to establish a union branch in all companies, or to join the appropriate union. However, trade union power has diminished over the years; only around ten per cent of the work force are members.

Membership is mainly strongest in the old industries of the north, such as steel, which have in themselves declined. New industries in the south, such as electronics, and those employing mainly women, do not have much union activity. This is by the choice of the employees.

The role of unions
Unions still have an important part to play, such as in the negotiation of the collective agreement. They are also less confrontational nowadays. Both the unions and the employers are more able to work together for the common good than in the past, though the relationship is by no means easy. Some of the functions of the unions are now also handled by the far more conservative works councils.

To join a union
See the local shop steward (délégué syndical) at your place of work. Foreigners are permitted to join and participate in all union activities.

Trades unions' rights
Trade union branches can be established in any company as a matter of right. Effectively, single union companies and single union deals are not permitted. However, companies seeking to achieve this, or even avoid union activity altogether, usually locate in an area which is favourable to this purpose.

The union branch may appoint a shop steward, who has a right to meet with the company management at least twice a year and make any appropriate representations. Companies with over ten employees can appoint one of their number as a délégué du personnel—an official whose task it is sort out problems in the workplace—quite apart from the shop steward.

Union officials have protected employment status (they cannot easily be dismissed) and must be given time during working hours to undertake their duties.

The main trades unions
The main trades unions in France, which in turn comprise numerous sectoral and regional federations, are:

- CGT: Confédération Générale du Travail. The largest and longest established union (1895). It operates mainly in old industries. Its leaders are Communist party members.

- CFDT: Confédération Française Democratique du Travail. Principally Socialist, it supports worker participation and ownership in industry.

- FO: Force Ouvrière. A moderate union with support in nationalised industries and the civil service.

- CFTG: Confédération Française des Travailleurs Chrétiens. The Christian Unionists, with a membership across many industries.

- CFE-CGC: Confédération Française de l'Encadrement de la Confédération Générale des Cadres. An executive union.

Other groups
There is also a right for employees to appoint special interest groups, quite separate from trades unions or works councils. Their job is to monitor any relevant matters such as health and safety or discrimination, and liaise with management. The whole idea of these groups is that they are discussion and consultation groups which avoid any form of confrontation.

Works councils
The works council (**Comité d'Entreprise**) is a comparatively new form of representative body which sometimes works parallel to the trades unions but occasionally operates in their place. Companies with over 50 employees must have a works council; it is not a choice as with unions.

Structure
Members of a works council are elected every two years and they are entitled to meet with the managing director of the company each month. Trades union officials are also entitled to participate in the works councils. However, works councils adopt a very conciliatory view and have become popular as a result. As with trades unions the council officials have protected status and time to undertake their duties.

Functions
Employees can take problems to the works council, which will raise them directly with management and try to reach a solution. However, management is not obliged to heed any of the council's recommendations. Matters commonly covered include pay, hours of work, health and safety.

Collective agreements
In recent years the most important function of the representative bodies has become the system of **collective agreements (Conventions Collectives)**. This highly formalised system for the negotiation of pay and conditions has proved reasonably effective. About 75 per cent of all jobs are paid at rates agreeed under collective pay-bargaining deals.

How the system works
Negotiations on pay, and also conditions, are undertaken annually and this involves negotiation between employers' organisations and trades unions or professional associations. The resultant agreement is binding on all employers and employees who are members of those organisations, though the agreement is also taken as an industry standard for those who are not.

Collective agreements do not apply to just one company. They can vary regionally and locally, cover all companies in a particular industry, or just different types of trade.

During the bargaining procedure pay rates, and also conditions of service, are renegotiated and agreed; nowadays both parties try to reach a consensus rather than become embroiled in a dispute. A standard rate of pay for a worker with average responsibilities in that industry is agreed and allocated a **coeffecient** of 100. The rate of pay is then calculated for employees who have more responsibilities and skills according to the coefficient which has been agreed for their job; for example coefficient 110 or 120.

Points you should be aware of
It is useful to be aware of the applicable pay coefficient when taking a job.

Also find out what Convention Collective applies to that particular company. The l'Inspection du Travail (labour inspector) in the local area can advise you. A copy of the appropriate Convention Collective can be obtained from:
Direction des Journaux Officiels
26 rue Desaix
75015 Paris
Tel: 1 40 58 75 00.
Details can also be obtained on the MINITEL system.

Possible problems
The pay-bargaining system usually works fairly effectively, with employers keeping to the terms and conditions their employer's organisations have agreed to. However, problems can occur when a company seeks to leave one Convention Collective and join another; perhaps one which has negotiated poorer terms and conditions.

Very important
One of the most important features of this system is that the rates of pay and conditions agreed are usually a minimum starting point. Many companies seek to improve on these as a recruitment incentive and also as a productivity bonus.

Strikes
The right to strike is guaranteed by the French constitution and so no-strike deals, like single-union deals, are largely not enforceable. Strikes (grèves) were common in France in the 1970s, but today there are fairly few and most are resolved quite quickly. The old industries of the north and the public sector are most vulnerable. Strikes are very rare in the new, high technology industries.

Information about the right to strike and the regulations which apply can be obtained from the local l'Inspection du Travail.

EQUALITY AT WORK

Working women
The number of women working in France has risen sharply in recent

years and this should continue. Reasons for this include the growth of high technology industries, which employ many female workers, and a growth in the popularity of part-time work amongst employers and employees. Most female workers are in their 20s and 30s; the proportion of women employed falls sharply above that age group.

Types of work
The work done by women falls into certain well-defined categories such as teaching, catering, health care and domestic work. In executive and professional work the number of women employed is much smaller than in the UK, although the female executives that do exist in France tend to be extremely competent and powerful—often head of a major department or company.

Equal rights
France has a commitment to equal opportunties. The Equal Pay Act 1972 and La Loi Rondy Sur l'Egalité Professionnelle (1983) were introduced to try to ensure this. However, the fact remains that the average female wage is still only around three-quarters of the average male wage. More women earn only the basic SMIC rate compared to men.

Some suggest that the current situation is due to the fact that fewer French women aspire to a career anyway. In any case this is bound to change as the women who have a career in mind start to reach the age where top jobs are within their experience. Foreign women may find that they are considered a breed apart and, having come to work in France, are automatically ambitious.

The attitude towards women in work is usually a mixture of chivalry and patronage. Women must work harder to achieve their desired position, but must still retain their femininity.

Child care
Facilities for working women, such as flexible working hours and crèches, are quite well developed especially in the newer industries and larger companies.

Ethnic minorities
Ethnic minorities fare poorly in pay and conditions, and unemployment within these groups is high. Many members of this community are involved in the black economy where SMIC rates and employment laws do not help them.

However, this applies mainly to the African and Eastern European workers in France, some of whom do not have the work permits which non-EC nationals must have. Invariably it is the case that western expatriates, including those from EC countries, can expect to be treated equally with French workers no matter what their sex or background.

WHERE DO YOU FIND OUT MORE?

Further queries about terms and conditions whilst working in France can be referred to:

- The Direction Départementale du Travail et de l'Emploi in the county town of your département of residence. See telephone directory.

- The local l'Inspection de Travail (labour inspector). See telephone directory.

Both these organisations can advise on employment law, including contracts, working hours, SMIC rates, redundancy and dismissal.

Information can also be obtained from a book called *Législation du Travail et Sécurité Sociale* (Editions Casteilla) which is stocked by most French bookshops and considered an authoritative guide to employment law.

CHECKLIST

Key points before accepting a job:

1. Check procedure for obtaining a residence permit.

2. Happy with terms and conditions of service and expectations of employers?

3. Review contract of employment. Ask for a specimen copy.

4. Check rates of pay are correct. (Refer to Convention Collective?)

5. Check terms and conditions are correct. (Refer to Convention Collective?)

6. Check position as regards trades unions and works councils. Do they operate? What help can they give?

7. Formulate a personal policy to deal with colleagues?

8. Women: likely problems and special considerations.

5
Guide to French Employment

DOES FRANCE NEED YOU?

Prior to the early 1980s France was a very insular country in employment terms. Most other major European countries were more accessible. French employers overwhelmingly wanted French workers, working to French standards; the majority of foreigners working in France were merely on short-term postings.

In the last decade, however, employers have begun to see the wisdom of recruiting abroad. Sometimes this is because foreign labour is cheaper. Mostly it is effectively a way of importing sought-after skills, which French industry needs if it is to succeed. Often, foreigners are employed to create footholds in their own national markets.

In short, the answer to the question whether France needs you is *yes!* However, with some exceptions, you will be employed because you have something the French employer wants. If you do not have that, expect finding a job to be harder. The flexibility of the Single European Market is important to the French, but no French employer recruits abroad for that reason alone.

Unemployment

Unemployment has become a persistent problem in France, making this country no escape from unemployment at home. Skilled and qualified foreign workers usually need to rely on their particular skills and qualifications to keep them employed. Management skills are also sought after.

With the exception of some technical fields, and executive posts, there is no general labour shortage in France. Some old industries are considered to be overstaffed. The best chances of finding work are in France's largest industries, especially the new sunrise industries which emerged in the 1980s.

The southern part of France is where most new jobs are being created, although Paris is still important.

Why recruit from the UK?

Of all the European countries French employers are keen to recruit from the UK. If not their first choice it is most definitely their second, after Germany. Reasons given for employing the British include their high level of competence, hard-working attitude and knowledge of British and world markets. French employers also know that, as pay is lower in the UK, the British employee may well be quite happy with a more modest salary!

WHAT JOB SHOULD YOU DO?

There is no reason why foreigners in France should not take any type of job, and certainly no laws to restrict what jobs you can take. This is, of course, subject to your having the necessary qualifications, skills and experience which are sought after by an employer. However, there are certain types of work which it is easier for foreigners to get in France, and for which they are more suited.

Selecting your approach

To stand the best chance of getting a job decide at the outset what is the best skill you can offer to a French employer. This usually means doing the same job you do now, or some other recent job, in France. You are unlikely to find many French employers will recruit you for anything else. In other words, find the best job on the market, not necessarily the one you would like. Being practical, a move to France is rarely a good time to start on a whole new career if you are to maximise your chances of finding a job.

This chapter covers the main French industries. These are the ones in which foreigners are more usually taken on because of the sheer numbers of people employed.

In other cases foreigners are employed *because* they are foreign. For example, in tourism, teaching and some commercial organisations you may be employed because you are a native English-speaker, and thus can help the employer deal with English-speaking customers.

THE MAIN TYPES OF WORK AVAILABLE

To simplify the job-finding procedure it is useful to consider the jobs available in three distinct caregories:
- **Professional**: Professional and executive people have a high status in France and in most cases earn substantially more than the average worker. They are particularly sought after in the new high-technology, technical and scientific industries rather than in, for example, private practice.

Cadre status is cherished in France and a great career advantage. It may be impossible for foreigners to obtain this status as it requires a particular background.

- **Skilled**: Skilled workers are very much the mainstay of the French workforce and found in all industries, from the old heavy engineering industries to computing and electronics. There is a shortage in some specific trades and limited geographic areas. Where available these jobs are more likely than any others to circulate in the EURES system.

    Much greater status is attached to being an **Ouvrier Qualifié** (a qualified skilled worker) than an ordinary skilled worker. It is important to have a record of vocational qualifications, training and career history.

- **Semi-skilled workers**: Semi-skilled workers are distinguished as being of a lower status by the term 'Ouvrier Spécialisé'.

- **Unskilled**: Those without any relevant qualifications can take unskilled jobs in France (whether permanently or for holiday work, etc). However, this is the most unemployment-ridden sector of the French jobs market and the most difficult to find work in.

    In the unskilled sector are many immigrant workers, especially from North Africa. Those seeking to take this type of work will encounter competition from those often willing to work unofficially for less than SMIC rates.

Decide now: What category of work are you looking for?

Jobs in the public sector

An alternative source of jobs
Traditionally, those seeking work in France aim to find work with private companies. This is realistic in that private companies have a commercial need to recruit from abroad. However, under EC regulations citizens of EC countries are entitled to seek work in the public sector of other EC states.

This may be an alternative worth considering, especially if you are employed in the public sector in the UK. However, the right under EC regulations does not remove the need to be skilled or qualified or speak the language.

Where could you work?
There are principally three fields of activity in the French public sector:

- Nationalised industries: Although some state industries have been privatised many are still in national ownership. Some are also France's largest companies, for example Renault, EDF (Electricité de France) and SNCF.

- Local authorities: As elsewhere, local authorities employ large numbers of people in local administration, highways, etc.

- Government service: France has a large and bureaucratic civil service, employing many in the operation of taxation, VAT, education and health.

Possibilities and potential
The EC regulations grant EC citizens the right to apply for and be appointed to jobs in the public sector on the same basis as any French national. The only jobs which you may be excluded from are those which are directly connected with national security or the exercise of public authority; you may not apply to become a Gendarme but most jobs with PTT (the Post Office) or SNCF (French railways) should be open.

It is not necessary to be a French national to take public sector jobs. In practice, however, it may not be easy to take advantage of this right. Early reports suggest that the public sector in France is reluctant to recruit foreign nationals. There is not presently any EC body to monitor operation of this right.

Renault	France Télécom
EDF (Electricité de France)	PTT
SNCF	Gaz de France
Air France	Docks de France
SEITA (Tobacco)	BNP (Banque National de Paris)
Crédit Lyonnais	Rhône-Poulenc
Pechiney	Aérospatiale

Fig 15. France's main nationalised companies

Where to find public sector jobs

- Write directly to public sector employers and ask for details of their recruitment procedures. Contacts can be obtained from the *Kompass France* directory (for nationalised industries) and the *European Municipal Directory* (for public authorities).

- The ANPE: Can help and advise, but only if in France.

- The CIO: The **Centre d'Information et d'Orientation** can advise on vacancies in the public sector. Check in the local telephone directory for the address of the nearest office.

- Newspapers: Some (but not all) vacancies are advertised. See the regional newspapers, listed in Chapter 2.

WHAT ARE THE MAIN INDUSTRIES?

Opportunities in commerce, business and industry

Being a major country France has examples of most industries and, generally, all the industries which exist in the UK exist in France. However, this section considers the biggest industries, which are also by definition the largest employers. These large industries will be some of the easiest to obtain employment in, by virtue of their size, and they are described here for that reason.

Some of the industries detailed here are also the areas in which foreigners are most readily employed. This particularly applies to the newer, high-technology industries which are more internationally orientated and so more inclined to recruit foreigners for the skills they can offer.

Aerospace

France is possibly the European leader in aerospace and has ambitions to become a major world force. It is one of the very few countries in the world to have its own civil and military aerospace and aeronautic products. However, France is closely linked with other European countries, especially Britain, in this respect.

The main companies are Aérospatiale and Airbus Industrie. The Airbus is one of the eight **Grands Projets** (prestigious projects which receive special Government encouragement). Thomson-CSF is a major world name in avionics. Generally, companies are out to recruit the best on the world market; language skills may be unnecessary in view of this.

Directions
Contacts with potential employers can be made through trade directories and professional associations. Jobs are also advertised in professional journals.

Agriculture

Agriculture has long been one of France's largest industries in terms of number of employees and also value of goods produced.

France is Europe's largest food producer and exporter (accounting for four per cent of GDP) and is largely self-sufficient.

French farms are generally not up to UK standards and are, on average, 60 per cent smaller than British farms, though they have improved somewhat over recent years. In Brittany and the Massif Central farms are often little more than subsistence smallholdings.

Farmers are trying to reconstruct; as a result there are job opportunities at all levels. British farmers are often secretly envied in France for their efficiency and successful use of modern technology. Those with qualifications may find they are sought after.

Directions
Local Chambres d'Agriculture, which exist in all towns in rural areas, can provide information and arrange contacts with farmers. Also see regional newspapers and the farmers' newspapers (and place advertisements there).

Banking, finance, insurance
Banking is currently not an activity in which France excels; the banking industry is smaller than in countries of similar world standing. Both Britain and Germany have more advanced financial markets and banking industries. France has aspirations to develop its industry, but Frankfurt not far across the border has always remained the main financial centre on mainland Europe. France opted for gradual updating of the financial markets, rather than the UK's 'Big Bang'.

Recent developments in French banking, including denationalisation of Société Générale, have led to steady growth in French financial institutions. It is likely this sector will grow in importance in future, with a resulting requirement for qualified and experienced staff. This pool of demand cannot easily be met from within France; suitable graduates and finance-orientated cadres are in short supply.

International banks and financial institutions are also very active within France, especially British institutions. Barclays is particularly active in the French market. Most opportunities are in Paris or Lyon, (France's second commercial city). There may be opportunities for posting.

Directions
The best approach is to make direct enquiries to financial institutions in the UK, France and Germany. Suitably qualified staff can approach recruitment consultancies. Most financial vacancies are advertised in *Les Echos*.

Chemicals

France has always boasted a very important chemicals industry. This has much to do with the country's very central and accessible position in Europe, and proximity to Germany and Switzerland. Currently most of the major companies involved are state-controlled, such as Rhône-Poulenc and Orkem. The Air Liquide company is one of France's largest companies.

Most spheres of interest are represented, including oil, petrochemicals, plastics, industrial gases, agrochemicals, biotechnology and, especially, pharmaceuticals. The centre of the industry is the Rhône valley. Shell and BP operate extensively, and other major names are Elf Aquitaine and Sanofi.

France does have a large oil and gas industry, though no significant reserves of its own. The company which dominates this, Elf Aquitaine, is France's largest company.

Directions
Direct approach to companies or recruitment agencies. See major newspapers and *l'Actualité Chimique* journal.

Consult chambers of commerce, as there are many small operators in the business.

Defence equipment

Apart from the UK and USA, France is the only country with a commercial defence manufacturing industry of any substantial size. This has been important for many years and some of the equipment, such as Mirage aircraft and Exocet missiles, have been great success stories in sales terms.

The French defence industry thrives upon the very substantial and often criticised French defence budget (15 per cent of all public spending). Aggressive marketing is carried out on a worldwide scale; French companies are very mercenary when it comes to promoting French products.

The companies involved specialise particularly in airborne fields, such as military aircraft and missiles, also electronics and computers. Thomson-CSF and Aérospatiale are major names. Only those with experience are likely to be recruited, but there is little secrecy and companies are anxious to recruit experts from around the world.

Directions
Professional associations and direct approaches are advised. Positions are highly specialised and rarely advertised on the open market.

Food processing

The French have been very successful in transforming a major national preoccupation into a booming export business; food products are now one of the largest contributors to the French economy (including FF20 billion in sales of wine annually). The largest and fastest expanding export market is the UK.

France is a major world producer of fruit, vegetables and cereal crops, despite the fact that farming techniques are generally not advanced. There is also a well-developed reputation for luxury, gourmet foods and drink. Processed foodstuffs, especially dairy products and confectionery, have started to penetrate German, Belgian, Dutch and UK markets. New markets are being aggressively pursued, and this is where much of the employment potential is.

The food and drink industry is expected to grow considerably, and is the subject of much Government encouragement and EC aid from the **EAGGF** and other **Structural Funds**. However, there is much competition from EC partners Spain, Italy, Portugal, Greece and Holland.

Many of the operators are little known; major names are BSN, LVMH, Nestlé, Nabisco and Béghin-Say.

Directions

As many of the operators are small companies try regional press, ANPE, trade directories such as *Kompass*. Also ask local chambre de commerce for contacts.

High-technology products

France has always had some heavy manufacturing industry, but its new direction is very much in high-technology. Much Government investment and commercial effort has been placed into the development and promotion of the manufacture of all kinds of products, using the most advanced and sophisticated technology available. Personnel are sought on a pan-European scale to make this industry a leader.

In the past many of the largest manufacturing companies were state owned. Some of these are now privatised and there is much more cooperation between Government and private industry to develop high technology; a result of the Filière Electronique programme of the 1980s. The south of France is a key area for these new industries, but encouragement has been given to starting them in Normandy and Brittany, areas of heavy industrial decline.

Electronics is a major part of this new industry; other specialities include robotics, automation, high-technology materials and high-technology manufacturing.

Directions
Due to the proliferation of small companies the trade directories (*Kompass France*) are the best reference. Also refer to professional journals and recruitment agencies.

Informatique
Informatique is very much an area of French pride. In British terms the description translates as computing but, more accurately, informatique encompasses every aspect of using technology to process, move and use data and information. Prior to 1980 the sector was almost exclusively dominated by the state. Now there are many major companies in these fields, including many international names. Hewlett Packard, IBM and Groupe Bull are the most prestigious names.

Computer companies operating in France are very strong in the area of software development. As English is the major language of the industry, also because many of the names involved are multinationals, there may be opportunities for suitably qualified 'informaticiens' (computer scientists), hardware engineers and marketing people. A majority of the informatique companies present in France (who are not Paris based) are located in the south of France; there is a flagship 'technopark' at Sophia Antipolis near Cannes.

Directions
Direct approach to companies is recommended, otherwise professional journals and recruitment agencies. EURES system may carry some difficult-to-fill specialist vacancies.

Iron, steel, aluminium
This is one of the old smokestack industries and, as in other countries, has reduced in size considerably over recent years. However, companies operating in this industry are still major employers and are continuing to redevelop the industry to meet the market conditions of the future, ie, more specialist steels, rather than bulk products. Subsequently, employment opportunities are likely to be in scientific and technical posts rather than shop floor.

Areas of most activity for iron, steel and aluminium are the north and north-east and the Marseille area.

Directions
Direct approach to companies is the most suitable method. Only small

numbers of jobs are advertised.

Motor manufacture

The manufacture of motor vehicles, principally cars, has long been an important French industry and this continues today. The industry has been transformed from a low point in the 1970s to become Europe's largest volume producer. French cars now account for 28 per cent of vehicles sold in Europe.

The two major names are Renault (state owned) and Peugeot-Citroën, with numerous plants and design facilities, principally in the north of the country. These companies also have interests all over Europe, with Peugeot-Talbot in the UK and plants in Spain, Portugal and Eastern Europe.

In addition to this, the motor components industry—typified by the enormous Michelin company—is still one of the country's largest employers.

Directions
Skilled and unskilled jobs through ANPE or regional/local newspapers. Skilled and professional personnel should also approach companies direct. *Kompass France* and chambers of commerce can provide contacts for the smaller companies.

Mining

France has some coal mining; this has much declined in recent years but is still important. Most mining activity is in the mining and recovery of iron ore (in the north) and bauxite and potash (in the south), and these are generally very modern and sophisticated industries.

In addition it is worth noting that although France has very few fossil fuel reserves of its own, it does have substantial industries in the import and processing of sources of fuel, such as oil, natural gas, coal, etc. France has some of the lowest industrial energy costs in Europe.

Directions
Direct approach to companies, newspaper advertisements and journals, principally *Mines et Carrières*. Some difficult-to-fill vacancies through EURES.

Pharmaceuticals

France is world famous as a producers of perfumes and cosmetics; not so well known for its considerable drug/pharmaceutical industry. The French are one of the largest users of drugs and cosmetics in the world. However, the second-largest users are the Germans for which the

French industry is conveniently situated! Products are being aggressively marketed to Switzerland, the UK and the USA (this has proved to be one of the best French export successes to North America).

There are likely to be employment opportunities in all spheres, not only pharmaceuticals but cosmetics and biotechnology. Some of the companies are large but family firms are surprisingly important. There are also many multinational partnership projects. The major names are Ciba-Geigy, Hoffman la Roche, L'Oréal, Merck, Roussel-Uclaf, Rhône-Poulenc, Synthêlabo, Sandoz.

Directions
Most methods are suitable, including reading newspapers and journals, ANPE, and using employment agencies. Also try direct approach to companies, using trade directories and chambers of commerce for leads.

Télématique

Télématique is considered a keystone industry in France. It encompasses rather more than just telecommunications; télématique covers the art of using telecommunications to provide effective communication by a host of different media. The French telecommunications industry is already the third largest in the world.

Areas of specialisation include telephone systems, cellular communications, satellite communications, fibre optics and cable networks. The Minitel communication system is one of the world's very few successful systems of its type.

Most of the companies involved are large organisations, some of them state owned and some of them multinational partnerships; there is much US involvement. Many of the companies are also active in other areas, such as computers, electronics and defence equipment. France Télécom is the nationalised industry responsible, but has been transformed by investment and deregulation in recent years. Other major players are CGE (Alcatel).

Directions
Direct approaches are recommended, together with use of newspapers and recruitment agencies.

The retail sector

In recent years retailing in France has changed out of all recognition. Previously a nation of small shopkeepers—as Napoleon once said of the British—retailing has developed on a big scale. Small, quality shops are still important to the French, but retailing, distribution and marketing have all grown fast in the last six to eight years.

France is now notable for its large number of efficient, well organised retailers, such as Carrefour and Leclerc, with hypermarkets nationwide. Some of them have started to expand overseas. Foreign companies have also started to enter the French market. There are likely to be job opportunities at all levels, from management to shop floor (where staff turnover is traditionally high).

- Mail order is a major business activity in France. There are several large mail order catalogue chains: La Redoute has interests in the UK.

- Fashion is a traditional French speciality; up to 70 per cent of production is for the lucrative export markets.

Directions
Most methods of finding a job can be used, especially newspapers, ANPE, employment agencies. Direct approaches may also be worthwhile and chambers of commerce can help with contacts.

The tourist sector

Although enthusiastically fostering new modern industry and high-technology, France is keen to promote the natural attributes of 'la belle France' by way of tourism. The industry is rooted around a substantial home market— few French people holiday abroad—but the country is also popular with other Europeans. Tourism typically earns FF300 billion per year.

Tourism operates summer and winter in France, with skiing in the Alps and summer tourism mainly along the south coast. However, almost all parts of France now benefit from tourist income.

The range of employment opportunities is very extensive. Although some executive-level jobs are available the vast majority of work is in semi-skilled and unskilled fields. Tourist work is ideal for holiday jobs or casual work; for many people something to fill in while you find a suitable permanent job. It is one of the few sectors where the unskilled can operate, perhaps with very little language knowledge.

Directions
Some jobs can be found by applying to UK package tour operators. However, most casual jobs are only available on the spot in France. Local newspapers, ANPE, temporary employment agencies and direct canvassing are the best methods.

Utilities

Just as in the UK where utilities have become big business in recent years, so they have in France. Private industry has had its impact (with Générale des Eaux, the water company) but there is still much state ownership. Not only are these industries important in their own right, but they have acted as a catalyst to other industrial development. Considerable improvements to the infrastructure took place in the mid-1980s and further developments, this time abroad, are expected in the early years of the Single European Market.

Areas of special interest are:

- Electricity. France has Europe's largest nuclear industry (with five times the capacity of that in the UK).

- Water services. Générale des Eaux is one of France's and Europe's leading companies. It is now involved in many other fields, often in high-technology areas. These include new energy sources, télématique and television.

Directions
Direct approach to major companies. Otherwise, newspapers, professional journals and ANPE.

OPPORTUNITIES FOR CASUAL WORK, HOLIDAY WORK AND WORKING EXCHANGES

Work experience in France

So far the openings in France have been discussed with a view to finding permanent employment there. However, most of the methods and opportunities discussed are also suitable for those who would like to work in France for a short period. These types of jobs are especially suitable for young people, and those who would like to try a taste of French life, perhaps before deciding on a permanent move.

Advantages
There are many advantages to casual or holiday jobs. You need no skills for most of them, anyone can apply. Often it is not necessary to speak much French (though it will always help). You can choose to work for a few months, or even just a few days.

Disadvantages
Disadvantages are that casual and holiday work may be hard, or dirty, or boring; a good way of telling if France is really for you. There are plenty of these jobs but competition for them, from immigrant

workers and students, is very high indeed.

How to find casual and holiday work
Casual and holiday jobs can sometimes be obtained from the UK, but it is invariably easier to travel to France and find work on arrival. The following methods should be considered:

- Local and regional newspapers: A major source of casual work, but be sure to respond immediately to the ads. Free newspapers (journals gratuits) are particularly suitable.

- ANPE: Are notified by employers of some casual and holiday jobs. Some officials are unwilling to help foreigners, especially if non-French-speaking. Try any seasonal offices: Agences Locales et Antennes Saissonnieres.

- Specialist agencies (UK): There are a number of specialist agencies in the UK which arrange casual work and exchange schemes. These particularly relate to au pairs/nannies and voluntary work. Further details on pages 115 and 116.

- Specialist agencies (France): There are also specialist agencies in France which can help arrange holiday and casual jobs. These mostly help students and young people, but all are prepared to help foreigners as well as French nationals.
  The main one is **CIDJ**, a youth and student organisation that can offer information and advice on travel, accommodation and finding casual jobs in France. Apart from the Paris office there are offices in all main cities which will help personal callers. CIDJ have a range of useful leaflets including *Recherche d'un Emploi Occasionnel* and *Entrée, Séjour et Emploi des Etrangers en France*. All are in French but understandable by those who have studied O level/GCSE French. CIDJ will send a free list of current titles on request.
  CIDJ (**Centre d'Information et de Documentation Jeunesse**)
  101 quai Branly
  75740 Paris Cedex 15.

- **CROUS:** The **Centres Régional des Oeuvres Universitaires et Scolaires** are not officially job agencies but, as employers tell them about vacancies they are often prepared to pass on information to students. It is necessary to call in person; look in the French telephone directories for their offices which are on campus at most French universities.

- **AJF**: The organisation **Accueil des Jeunes en France** principally offers advice on cheap accommodation and travel, but also sometimes knows of job opportunities.
  AJF
  12 rue Barres
  75004 Paris.

- Writing letters: Writing letters to potential employers in France can result in the offer of a holiday job, but the chances are very limited as most employers can take their pick from those who turn up on the spot. Some job seekers have been successful by writing to hotels and restaurants (addresses from tourist guides) or to farmers, etc. (For further tips and advice see Chapters 2 and 3.)

- Personal calling: Personal calling is one of the best ways of getting work, although knocking on doors (hotels, restaurants, shops, farms, etc) can be hard and disappointing work and most employers receive many more offers of work than they can use.

- Private employment agencies: The temporary employment agencies, as covered in Chapter 2, offer temporary work to students and casual workers. Indeed, strictly they are only allowed to offer temporary work by law. However, you must usually speak good French to use them. The agencies in Paris are often short of workers in July and August, when residents go off on holiday for up to a month and temporary workers are needed in shops, hotels, restaurants and factories etc. Some agencies are listed on page 147.

Pay and conditions
Pay and conditions can be poor for holiday work and casual jobs. Sometimes it is black work: paid in cash, no questions asked. However, all reputable employers will pay SMIC rates (sometimes SMIC + ten per cent). Employment may only be by the day or the week, which may depend on how long the harvest or tourist season, etc, happens to last that year.

Perks
Some casual jobs provide accommodation and food (**Logement et Nourriture Assurés**) free or at a moderate cost.

Important
Offers of casual work should always be carefully scrutinised. Occasionally, there are unscrupulous employers or agencies who charge a fee with the promise of a job which never materialises, making inflated deductions for accommodaton, or promise commission on sales which is unrealistic.

Organisations like CIDJ are usually prepared to advise on pay and conditions.

MAIN TYPES OF CASUAL AND HOLIDAY WORK IN FRANCE

Tourism

The potential
The tourist industry in France employs tens of thousands of casual workers each year, creating an enormous demand for manpower. However, as jobs in tourism initially seem the most romantic, and rates of pay are some of the highest, there is a lot of competition for every single job.

The tourist industry in France conveniently divides into two: in summer (from June to September) it is mostly along the south coast. In winter the tourists go skiing in the Alps (December–April).

What jobs are available?
Many different types of work are available, most require no prior skills. Most are in tourist facilities such as hotels and restaurants. Hotels require porters and chambermaids. Bars and restaurants require bar staff, waiters, washers-up and kitchen porters. If you can speak good French you may get reception work, or a job in a shop. If you can play an instrument you might get work as an entertainer. Good sportsmen and women may get jobs as instructors (though not skiing, which is virtually a closed shop).

One of the main types of job for those from the UK is that of courier, maintenance hand or entertainer on one of the many camp sites in the south of France.

How to get jobs
If seeking work on a camp site, write to the package tour operators in the UK in the autumn of the previous year. See their brochures at travel agents. For jobs in hotels/bars/restaurants you could try writing speculative letters between March and May. Obtain addresses from one of the many tourist guides on France.

It is, however, best to apply in person once in France, simply by going from door to door of likely looking establishments. ANPE may help, but cannot be relied on. If you can speak French private employment agencies are the best source of jobs.

Agriculture

The potential
Farming is a major French industry and it is largely quite labour intensive compared to the UK or Germany. As a result demand for casual labourers is high; France is home to many gipsies and travelling workers who move around following the harvests. The French grape harvest (known as the **Vendange**) attracts casual workers from all over Europe in September and October.

Most of these jobs need no knowledge of French. However, if you can claim some previous knowledge of farming, horticulture or animal care it will be much easier to get a job. Disadvantages are that the pay is low and the work hard. Many labourers work 12-hour days and pay may be linked to the amount of fruit picked, etc.

What jobs are available?
Work in agriculture is varied, many people are employed to harvest crops such as grapes, apples, pears, cherries, etc. Mechanisation has cut the number of jobs and the Vendange usually has a surplus of would-be pickers. Most farmers will employ workers to do planting, weeding, milking and tractor driving and many also expect their workers to do jobs around the house.

Most French farmers (or more usually smallholders) demand hard work. Many are quite poor and can pay only small wages. Sometimes they offer accommodation as part of the payment.

How to get jobs
It is occasionally possible to get jobs on farms by writing speculative letters, but this stands only a very slim chance of succcess. The Chambre d'Agriculture in the area where you wish to work may pass on contacts.

Not all casual farming jobs are notified to ANPE. However, a sister organisation of CIDJ can help and advise:
Sesame
9-11 square Gabriel Fauré
75017 Paris
Tel: 1 40 54 07 08.

CROUS offices may also help students.
Ideally, application should be made direct to farmers and

smallholders in person. Again the Chambre d'Agriculture may help. In wine-producing areas the local tourist office or SICA (wine producers' association) may provide directions and/or lists of vineyards.

Au pair and nannying

The potential
Au pair and nannying work has attracted foreign workers to France since the early 1800s. This type of work is just as popular today and, unlike in the past, those from other EC countries have an advantage in that no work permit is required, unlike those from other countries.

There is an important difference between au pair and nannying work. Au pairs are mostly inexperienced people, 18-27 at most, who live as part of a family for a period, usually one year, and help with child care. Nannies usually need to be qualified or well experienced; they can be any age and it is a full-time career job.

Au pairs and nannies are almost always female. A few men can find jobs in France, but it is very rare.

What will you do?
A nanny often has sole charge of the children and looks after them as her own. She is paid a good wage (in France this may be FF70,000-120,000 per year) and usually (but not always) has to live in.

An au pair lives as part of the family and accommodation is always provided. She is not paid a wage, but pocket money (likely to be around FF2,000 per month). Au pairs may be expected to enter in to a **fixed term contract** (an **Accord de Placement Au Pair d'Un Stagiaire Aide Familial** with the family and may be required to study French or some other subject in evening classes.

How to get jobs
One of the advantages of this type of work is that it can be obtained in the UK; numerous agencies offer to arrange placements (most charge a fee). In the case of au pairs these are often organised programmes with transport, a host family arranged, insurance, etc. Some agencies are listed below.

There are also several charitable organisations in France which arrange au pair placements. These include Accueil Familial des Jeunes Etrangers, Alliance Française and Services de Jeunesse Féminine.

Nannies should consult ANPE or the private French employment agencies, especially if they speak some French. Both nannies and au pairs should see newspaper advertisements once in France; an alternative is to place a Situations Wanted ad, but proceed with caution. In Paris jobs are advertised on bulletin boards, including the one at the British Council, 9-11 rue Constantine.

Contacts

Anglia Au Pair and
 Domestic Agency
37 Old Southend Road
Southend on Sea
Essex SS1 2HA
Tel: (0702) 613888.

Avalon Agency
30 Queens Road
Brighton
E. Sussex BN1 3XA
Tel: (0273) 26866.

Alliance Française
101 boulevard Raspail
75006 Paris.

Helping Hands Au Pair and
 Domestic Agency
10 Hertford Road
Ilford
Essex IG2 7HQ
Tel: (081) 597 3138.

Accueil Familial des
 Jeunes Etrangers
23 rue Cherche-Midi
75006 Paris.

Comité Parisien de
 l'Association Catholique des
 Services de Jeunesse Feminine
65 rue Monsieur le Prince
75006 Paris.

Voluntary/charity work

The potential
If you do not have to do paid work to support your stay in France then voluntary or charity work might be a solution. This pays no wage of course, but it offers a chance to get to know France in a way that those tied to paid employment cannot. In fact some charity work does pay a small wage or pocket money, and accommodation and food is usually provided free.

There are largely four different types of voluntary or charity work:

- archaeology
- conservation
- work with children (such as in summer camps)
- work with the old, disabled or poor.

What is involved?
Charity and voluntary work comes in many forms, but it is usually hard, dirty or demanding. For example, you could become involved with a scheme to repair mountain footpaths, or renovating an old

building to form a day centre for elderly people. If you have a relevant skill, such as a manual trade or a first aid certificate, then it is a good idea to make this clear. Knowledge of French is useful but rarely essential.

If you do have a skill then you may find yourself leading a project and being put in charge of other workers. If not, it is usually a case of being a hired hand: for example, clearing out ditches or taking disabled children on an outing.

Most of the work is in summer (June-August). Application should be made early; start looking as soon as February.

How to get jobs
The vast majority of this type of work is arranged by special organisations, voluntary work agencies or charities. It is easiest to use those located in the UK, but you can approach agencies, etc, direct in France if you speak some French. Some of the main agencies are listed next but full, current details are given in the annual directory *Working Holidays* published by the Central Bureau for Educational Visits and Exchanges.

The most popular programmes are always over-subscribed; they rarely take all comers and you must usually show some dedication to the cause in question.

Contacts
International Voluntary Service
162 Upper New Walk
Leicester LE1 7QA
Tel: (0533) 549430.

Christian Movement for Peace
Bethnal Green United
  Reformed Church
Pott Street
London E2 0EF
Tel: (071) 729 1877.

Association Paralyses
  de France
17 boulevard Auguste-Blanqui
75013 Paris.
Projects working with the
  handicapped.

British Trust for Conservation
  Volunteers
36 St Marys Street
Wallingford OX10 0EU
Tel: (0491) 39766.

United Nations Association
International Youth Service
Temple of Peace
Cathays Park
Cardiff CF1 3AP
Tel: (0222) 223088.

Etudes et Chantiers
  International
33 rue Campagne Première
75015 Paris.
Conservation projects.

Jeunesse et Reconstruction
10 rue de Trevise
75009 Paris.
Conservation/restoration projects.

The International Movement
107 avenue du Général Leclerc
95480 Pierrelaye.
Work with the poor.

Association Montaigne
83 boulevard de Montmorency
75016 Paris.
Paid work on children's summer camps, sporting qualifications preferred.

CIDJ can also help and advise.

Exchange programmes

The potential
Exchange programmes offer a very different type of work. They are essentially for students or those in employment in the UK who want to gain work experience in France. This may be with a view to working there—some exchangees are offered permanent jobs—but it is not essential.

Exchanges can be undertaken at any age but they are principally for those aged 18-30. It is usually necessary to be already engaged in a course of study, be qualified, or be experienced in a particular field which is appropriate to the exchange programme.

Some exchanges pay a wage, others provide only accommodation. On that basis all offer a chance to experience work in France and, if you so wish, make contacts or arrangements for a permanent job in future.

What will you do?
Some exchanges are literally that: you swap jobs with someone who performs the same work as yourself in France. However, this is not necessarily the case; sometimes you may merely shadow a French worker, but not exchange with them. Some other exchange schemes are akin to apprenticeship schemes—or **Stages** as they are known in France.

Language experience is not always essential, but is preferable.

How to find an exchange scheme
Exchange schemes are organised by specialist organisations. A degree of detective work may be needed to track them down. The following sources of information can be tried:

- Your employer. Some may know of suitable schemes, organised under the **Scope** programme.

- Your university or college.

- French Embassy
  Cultural Section
  23 Cromwell Road
  London SW7.
  The Cultural Section knows of several schemes and can provide further contacts.

- The Commision of the European Communities
  8 Storey's Gate
  London SW1P 3AT.
  Tel: (071) 973 1992.
  The Commission has a **Stagiaire** scheme which may have places in France.

- The Central Bureau for Educational Visits and Exchanges
  Seymour Mews House
  Seymour Mews
  London W1H 9PE
  Tel: (071) 486 5101.
  The Central Bureau acts as an agent for several exchange schemes.

Each organisation will supply details of the exchanges they are involved with, together with the terms and conditions for eligibility.

Alternatives
If an exchange programme relevant to your interests does not currently operate then it is possible to apply for funding under the **Young Workers Educational Programme (YWEP)** or **Youth Exchange Programme**, either as an individual or a group, to create your own exchange scheme. Details can be obtained from the Central Bureau (above).

FRANCE BY REGIONS

Commerce and industry are not spread evenly across France. Some regions have examples of all industries but, usually, different areas specialise in different activities. Below is an overall guide to what industries, and hence what types of jobs, predominate in the regions of France.

Alsace
Mining, mineral exploitation, engineering, brewing, motor manufacture.

Aquitaine
Tourism, wine production, trading, electronics. Bordeaux is a major aerospace and aviation city.

Auvergne
Agriculture, light and heavy engineering.

Brittany
Agriculture, motor manufacture, télématique, printing, publishing, food processing.

Burgundy
Food production, wine production, agriculture, iron and steel, engineering, motor manufacture.

Champagne-Ardenne
Mining, engineering, agriculture, wine production (Champagne).

Corsica
Tourism, agriculture.

Côte d'Azur
Tourism, electronics, informatique, high-technology manufacturing.

Franche-Comte
Light and heavy engineering, mining, textiles, agriculture.

Languedoc
Agriculture, electronics, computing, scientific equipment, research and development, télématique, tourism.

Limousin
Agriculture.

Loire Valley
Agriculture, food processing, wine production.

Western Loire
Fishery, agriculture, shipping, food processing, electronics, télématique.

Lorraine
Electronics, computers, finance, banking, textiles, agriculture, food processing.

Nord-Pas de Calais
Engineering, steel, mining/minerals, electronics, transport, utilities.

Normandy
Heavy engineering, motor manufacture, chemicals, pharmaceuticals, agriculture, télématique, tourism.

Paris region
Business and administration, banking, finance, motor manufacture, heavy and light manufacturing, tourism, agriculture.

Picardy
Iron and steel, textiles, engineering, agriculture.

Poitou-Charentes
Agriculture, fisheries.

Provence
Heavy industrial, oil, textiles, chemicals, iron and steel, engineering, shipping, transport, informatique, aerospace, electronics, agriculture, tourism.

Pyrénées
Agriculture, electronics, research and development. Toulouse is a major aerospace and aviation centre.

Rhône
Business and administration, chemicals, textiles, heavy engineering, motor manufacture, agriculture, high-technology industries.

Savoy and Dauphiny
Engineering, mining, minerals, textiles, tourism, electronics, scientific equipment, télématique, informatique, nuclear industry.

CHECKLIST

1. Am I looking for professional, skilled or unskilled work?
2. Can I fit into one of the main French industries?
3. Which area of France do I prefer/is best for the industry I plan to work in?
4. Should I consider a job in the public sector?
5. Should I take a holiday or casual job as a taster of France?

6
Relocating to France

MOVING YOUR HOME TO FRANCE

Taking your personal possessions

What are the possible problems?
After 1 January 1993 there is free movement of goods through all EC countries. However, the situation is unclear at the time of writing.

The rates of VAT charged are still different in the UK and France and, despite the Single European Market, each EC country is still allowed to charge their own VAT on goods imported in certain circumstances, ie if they are new or nearly new and imported by a non-VAT registered person.

What are your rights?
You are entitled to import all your personal possessions, household furniture and household effects into France, and indeed any EC country, without having to pay import taxes or duties. It is as well to follow the procedure which has been operative for several years in order to ensure your possessions qualify for tax-free admission. The regulations under which this can be done are that:

- You are moving permanently to France.
- The items are at least three months old.
- The items must all be imported within 12 months of first arriving.

Things to check
Details of the current procedure should be checked with the French Consulate. However, you will probably require:

- Your passport.
- An inventory of all goods taken (two original copies).
- A copy of your contract of employment (or Carte de Séjour if already obtained).

- Attestation of previous residence in the UK. (A UK solicitor can provide this for a small fee.)

Present these to customs or police at the port of entry when moving to France. No prior consent or certificate is needed.

UK VAT
There are three bands:
- exempt
- zero per cent
- 17.5 per cent.

French VAT
There are four bands:
- exempt
- 7 per cent reduced rate (food, etc)
- 18.6 per cent standard rate (most goods)
- 28 per cent luxury rate (cars, etc).

Further information
Further information on importing goods is available from the French Consulate.

Taking your car to France
You have a right to import your own car into France without payment of any duties or taxes. The conditions which apply to this are that:

- The car must not be new.
- It must have been registered in your name for six months.
- It must be registered duty-paid in another EC country.
- Only one car per person is permitted duty-free and commercial vehicles are not eligible.

Add the vehicle to the inventory as above and present with your registration document and proof of ownership (a receipt or invoice should suffice) at the port of entry.

Although free movement of goods is possible within the EC this will not apply to cars until 1997. French VAT may be charged on vehicles which do not qualify as above.

Using your car in France
Bear in mind that your UK car will be right-hand drive in a left-hand drive country. Yellow headlamps are no longer compulsory, but advisable. A GB plate is still required for your vehicle until it is re-registered.

Once resident in France your car must be re-registered with a French registration number and fitted with French number plates. Do this at the local mairie using the form 846A which should be given to you at the port of entry. You will supplied with a French registration document (**Carte Grise**) and have to purchase a French road tax sticker (**Vignette**) from the local Centre des Impôts.

In order to register your vehicle it will require a roadworthiness test; have this done at the Service des Mines.

Insurance

Your UK home and motor insurance are usually only valid as long as you are a UK resident, in respect of your car, and a French home is usually only covered on UK insurance if it is a holiday home (and then, not necessarily). Once resident you will need to arrange French insurance.

Insurance can be arranged by contacting a **compagnie d'assurance** (see *Yellow Pages*).

Further information
Information on insurance can be obtained from:
CDIA (Centre de Documentation et d'Information de l'Assurance)
2 rue de la Chaussée d'Antin
75009 Paris
Tel: 1 42 47 90 00.
Information is also given on Minitel (Access Code 36 14 CDIA).

Driving licences

A UK driving licence is valid in France, as it stands, for up to 12 months after arrival. However, if you are resident in France (with a Carte de Séjour) it is preferable that you keep a French translation with it.

Within 12 months you must exchange your UK licence for a French **Permis de Conduire**. This can be done at the local préfecture or commissariat de police. You will require:

- translation of your UK licence
- Carte de Séjour
- Three photographs.

If your proposed job involves driving do check in advance as minimum driving ages and vehicle groups are not the same in France, even though EC countries use the same driving licence form.

Further information
Information on driving licences is available from the French

Consulates or the Service du Permis de Conduire at a main police station in France.

LEARNING THE LANGUAGE

Do I need to speak French?

If moving to any other country, such as Germany or Spain, you might just get by with a very basic knowledge of the relevant language. In France this is not really the case: you will be at a major disadvantage if you cannot speak French.

Not all French people speak English. Some do but refuse to use it. Only in a few casual jobs can you genuinely get by without speaking French.

In some areas such as Brittany and Languedoc you may encounter strange local dialects which may take some getting used to, but standard French is spoken everywhere.

Learning French
Consider the following methods:

- Audio cassette courses: Usually inexpensive, but there is no opportunity to practice. Obtain from bookshops. Courses offered by organisations such as Linguaphone are more comprehensive but more costly.
  Linguaphone
  124 Brompton Road
  London SW3 2TL

- Evening classes: Inexpensive, but usually aimed at holiday-makers. For details refer to your local further education college.

- Commercial schools: A quick way to learn but costly and mainly for business people; for details see *Yellow Pages*; for example, Berlitz.

- Institut Français: The French cultural centre in London offers crash courses (two weeks, currently £280) and intensive courses (four weeks, currently £310). Details from:
  Institut Français
  14 Cromwell Place
  London SW7 2DT
  Tel: (071) 581 2701.

- Residential courses in France: These are held at most French

Relocating to France

universities during the summer vacation. Contact the most convenient university direct.

- Commercial schools in France: A quick way to learn but will cost more than in the UK. Several schools are run by:
  Berlitz International
  79 Wells Street
  London W1A 3BZ
  Tel: (071) 637 0330.
  Or contact direct in Paris: 1 40 74 00 17.

FINDING A HOME

General information

Availability
It is always advisable to find a home before leaving to take up your job. That said, accommodation in France is fairly plentiful and reasonably priced, except perhaps in Paris and the Côte d'Azur. Temporary accommdoation in a hotel is usually reasonably priced—if you are in a hurry to move—except in luxury establishments.

Getting help
Few French employers will provide accommodation, but some will pay towards it if in an expensive area, such as Paris, one where it is difficult to find accommodation, or in the not-so-popular areas where it is hard to attract staff. Executive-level staff could expect assistance anywhere outside Paris as French executives are often unwilling to step off the Paris career ladder. You must ask for assistance and benefits; they will rarely be offered.

Casual workers in hotels or on farms will very often receive live-in accommodation.

What are costs and rents like?

France has a reputation for having cheap property and it is indeed generally cheaper than in the UK. Paris and desirable areas of large cities (especially Lyon, Toulouse, Grenoble and Bordeaux) can be dearer, or no cheaper than the UK. The bargains advertised in the UK (£5,000 for a cottage) are usually in very remote areas.

- Typical price for a three-bed house to buy: £50,000.
- Typical price for a two-bed apartment to rent: £300/month.

How do you find accommodation?
Accommodation to purchase and rent can be located by:

- Using an estate agent (an **agent immobilier**). Refer to the *Yellow Pages*. French estate agents are generally very reputable.
- Classified advertisements, see column entitled Immobilier, in local and regional newspapers.
- UK property magazines, such as *Living France* and *France*, at newsagents. Usually feature more costly property in rural locations.
- *Lagrange Anglais*. A French property magazine. Available on subscription:
    64 rue du Ranelagh
    75016 Paris.
    Tel: 1 45 24 33 33.

Points about purchase

Legal assistance
The property purchase procedure is very different from that in the UK. You do not necessarily need a lawyer, either British or French, to assist, as all property conveyancing is done by the **notaire**, a French official who handles the sale for both buyer and seller. However, you may find it useful to have your own lawyer to advise; several willing firms can usually be found advertising in *Living France* or *France*.

Contracts and costs
The most important points to note are that once an offer is made and accepted a deposit is paid and neither buyer nor seller can cancel the deal. Contracts are prepared by the notaire, who acts for both parties. There are not separate solicitors as in the UK. Professional fees and transfer taxes could easily add 15 per cent to the purchase price; in a few areas the buyer pays the estate agency fees also.

Points about rental
Property rented after 23 December 1986 is covered by **la Loi Méhaignerie**. Under this law:

- Leases must be for at least three years.
- A bond and deposit may be demanded but this must not exceed two months' rent.
- You are entitled to a formal lease document. You cannot be evicted unless you breach this.

- Rent can only be reviewed once a year and only increased by a prescribed amount.
- Service charges can be made; these are often shared between tenants, where the property is in a block.

Further information
Further information on property matters can be obtained from:
ANIL (Association Nationale Pour l'Information Sur le Logement)
2 boulevard St Martin
75010 Paris.
Tel: 1 42 02 05 05.

SOCIAL SECURITY IN FRANCE

Social security in the EC

The social security system throughout the EC is already well integrated and has been for several years. The main advantage of the system is that it is portable. Your social security contributions in one EC country entitle you to social security benefits in another.

As long as your social security contributions record is fully paid up in any one of the EC countries you will be entitled to social security benefits in any of the others. So, for example, if you work in the UK and then move to France to work you can claim French benefits from your UK record. If you then move back to the UK you can claim UK benefits based on your UK and French contributions.

Registering for social security

Check with your employer
Once working in France your employer is responsible for registering you with the social security scheme called **Sécurité Sociale**. You will receive a card with a social security number.

Eligibility
All French benefits require a minimum number of hours worked to be eligible. In the case of medical treatment (soins de santé) you must have worked 200 hours during the past three months. However, if you have worked these in the UK they will count towards your elegibility. Obtain Form E104 from the Department of Social Security (DSS) Oveseas Branch in Newcastle to prove this, if appropriate, and hand it to your employer who will pass it on to Sécurité Sociale.

What benefits are available?
The range of social security benefits in France includes:

- sickness, maternity, invalidity benefits;
- a death insurance scheme;
- old-age and invalidity pensions;
- family benefits;
- unemployment benefits.

When do you become eligible?

As soon as you receive your Carte de Séjour you must ensure you are registered for Sécurité Sociale and start paying national insurance contributions (**Cotisations à la Sécurité Sociale**). Contributions are payable by both employee and employer and are deducted from your salary. You and your dependants then become eligible for all the French benefits, as any French person. Medical treatment (but no other benefits) are available to those staying in France but not yet resident (see later).

Important exception
If you are only staying in France for a period of up to 12 months (occasionally longer), and are working for a company based outside France, then you can stay covered by UK Social Security and continue to pay National Insurance contributions in the UK. Obtain Form E101 from the Department of Social Security in the UK and present it to the French Sécurité Sociale to claim exemption from paying French contributions.

Rates of benefit

Some social security benefits in France are paid at a fixed rate. However, many are paid at a fixed rate plus a percentage of your former salary. For example, unemployment benefit is paid at a fixed daily rate plus 42 per cent of your former salary for a limited period (12 months at the very most).

How to claim benefits

Unemployment benefits (Chômage)
1. Register at the local ANPE.
2. Make a claim with the local office of **ASSEDIC** (Association for Employment in Industry and Trade).

Health and sickness benefits
Most benefits are dealt with by your local **Caisse Primaire d'Assurance Maladie**. See telephone directories for contacts.

Transferring unemployment benefit

Your rights
Those employed in the UK can transfer their unemployment benefit to France, and indeed other EC countries, whilst living there and looking for a job. This is possible if you have been claiming benefit for four weeks or more in the UK. In order to do this ask your unemployment benefit office for Form E303. If going only to France there is no need to nominate a specific place in France where you will claim.

What to do
On arrival in France go to any ANPE office and register for work and unemployment benefit. You can then receive benefit at the UK rate for up to three months. If you claim within seven days of arrival you will not lose any benefit.

Possible problems
The drawback of this system is that very few ANPE offices know about this system. Even those that do are not very cooperative. You will need to be persistent—and do not expect the ANPE staff to speak any English!

Once you have taken advantage of this facility you cannot repeat it unless you spend a period working back in the UK.

Child benefit
If you are receiving child benefit, and take advantage of the transfer of unemployment benefit, your child benefit can usually still be paid while you are in France looking for work whether your children accompany you or stay in the UK. Ask the DSS Child Benefit Centre (Washington), Newcastle Upon Tyne NE88 1AA for details.

Sickness benefits
If you become ill whilst in France looking for work then UK sickness benefit can usually be paid so long as your entitlement to unemployment benefit lasts. Contact the nearest Caisse Primaire to claim.

Medical treatment
Whilst in France looking for work and claiming UK unemployment benefit, you and your family are entitled to French medical insurance benefits which will cover most (but not all) the cost of medical treatment as discussed in the next section. Obtain a Form E119 from the DSS to prove this.

Further information

Further information can be obtained from:
Department of Social Security (DSS)
Overseas Branch
Newcastle Upon Tyne NE98 1YX.

Ask for booklet SA29 and the EC booklet *Social Security for Migrant Workers – France*.

HOSPITALS AND HEALTH PROVISION

How does the system work?

Standards
Health treatment in France is at least as good as in the UK. There is not a national health service as in the UK, in that treatment is not free at the point of use. However under the Sécurité Sociale system most treatment is subsidised. *It is not always free.*

Registration
Your employer will register you for Sécurité Sociale. Once registered you are entitled to equal treatment to French nationals. You may choose your own doctor, dentist and hospital.

Possible problems
Some French doctors and nurses do speak some English but this is by no means widespread. The local British Consulate should be able to advise you where English-speaking facilities are available.

How to get treatment

The system
All hospitals, doctors and dentists in France run on a commercial fee-charging basis. Some are privately run, others are trusts but still fee-paying. Many but not all of them agree to charge rates set by the Sécurité Sociale system. These are known as **Conventionnés**.

The procedure
If you need a hospital, doctor or dentist you can go to any. However, if they are **non-conventionnés** they can charge whatever they like and you may not be able to reclaim any of this. If the facilities are conventionnés then their fees will be covered by social security.

On receiving treatment you must usually pay for it yourself, unless in case of in-patient treatment in which case you pay only a small proportion.

On completion of treatment you will be given a receipt (a **Feuille de Soins**). Send this to the local **Caisse Primaire d'Assurance Maladie** and your costs will be refunded.

Important
In most cases social security does not pay all the cost of treatment (except for major operations or very costly drugs). For example:

- minor operations are only reimbursed at 80 per cent;
- most drugs are only reimbused at 70 per cent;
- doctors'/dentists' fees are reimbused at 75 per cent.

Hence, there is a contribution to make. However, many employees have a top-up scheme provided by their employer as a perk, with a **Mutuelle** insurance organisation. This will pay the balance to make the treatment effectively free.

Take Form E111
If staying in France, but not resident, you cannot automatically get free medical treatment. However, Form E111, which is available from main post offices in the UK, will entitle you to use the French health care system as above. Present the E111 to Conventionnés doctors or hospitals and they will charge the prescribed rates.

After treatment obtain the receipts and send them to the Caisse Primaire. They will refund your outlay, less the part that the patient pays, as above. You can, if you wish, take private insurance to bridge the gap.

If you do not have an E111 you will have to pay either Conventionnés or Cliniques Privées rates and will not usually be able to claim these back.

MONEY AND BANKS

Importing and exporting money
Money can be imported or exported to and from France without limit. There is no longer any exchange control.

Opening a bank account
To open a bank account in France simply call into any French high street bank and open one. In addition, the French banks Crédit Agricole and Société Générale have London offices. It is important to open an account at an early stage; most salaries may only be paid by cheque (**Cheque**) and some are paid by credit transfer (**Virement Bancaire**).

Facilities
Both cheque and savings accounts are available. Cheque accounts do not pay interest but do levy account charges. You will receive a cheque book, there are no cheque cards in France, and also a card for use at cash dispensers (**GAB** machines). Your accounts can be managed and bills paid by using the Minitel system.
Mortgages are obtainable in France on similar terms to the UK. However, unsecured loans are rarely offered without a satisfactory banking record. Each individual is entitled to have a tax-free savings account, similar to a TESSA.

Important
It is a serious offence in France to issue a cheque if having insufficient funds to cover it. If this is done your account may be frozen.

Further information
All the main UK banks have expatriate departments which can advise on banking and financial arrangements for expatriates. Addresses are in the Further Information section, page 142.

INCOME TAX

How do French tax levels compare to British?
In general, typical French tax rates are higher than the UK and range between 5 per cent and 56 per cent of income; the system operates on a sliding scale.
Having said this, many French employers will pay less than a taxpayer in similar circumstances in the UK. This is because of the wide range of allowances: social security contributions, some mortgage interest, insurance premiums, child care expenses and the wages of domestic staff may all be claimed as allowances.

Social security
The impact of social security contributions—typically 18 per cent of salary—is regularly criticised and should not be underestimated.

Dealing with taxation

Registering
It is advisable to register with the local tax authorities when you arrive. Do not assume the employer will do it. The address of the appropriate Centre des Impôts can be found in the local telephone directory.

Tax returns
An annual tax return must be filed for each tax year: the tax year is the same as the calendar year in France. This should be sent to the Centre des Impôts after 1 March following the year which it covers.

Payment
After filing the tax return a bill will be received. This can then be paid in three instalments, although it is also possible to pay monthly. Payment is made to the **Trésor Public**.

If working in France for the first time then, in the first year of earning, tax will not be payable until the September following the end of the first tax year worked. Subsquently you will follow the three-instalment or monthly system.

Non-residents
Non-residents must usually have income tax deducted at source by their employer. A return will then have to be filled in as above and any under- or over-payment adjusted. Your tax affairs will be dealt with by the **Centre des Impôts des Non Résidents**, rather than the local **Centre des Impôts**.

Leaving the UK Inland Revenue behind

UK taxation
Leaving the UK and working in France does not necessarily allow you to automatically escape UK tax. You can be physically resident and earning your income in France but still regarded as resident in the UK for tax purposes by the Inland Revenue.

In order to cease to be liable to UK tax you usually have to:

- Be based abroad for at least one full UK tax year.
- Not return from the UK for more than three months in any one year.
- Be employed in work that is wholly undertaken abroad (business trips back to UK are allowed).
- Not have property available for your use in the UK.

However, situations vary and it is advisable to check your individual situation with the Inland Revenue before leaving.

French taxation
Being employed in France automatically brings you within the scope of French taxation, regardless of the amount earned or how short the

period of work is. If not working you become liable to French taxation after a stay of 183 days within any one calendar year.

Double taxation
There is a double taxation agreement between the UK and France. The principles of double taxation mean that if you have income in both countries (for example, a wage in France and bank interest in UK), you will not have to pay tax twice on the same income—once each in both countries—but only in the country where you are considered resident or where the income arises.

Further information
Further information should be obtained from your local Inland Revenue Office (see telephone directory). Ask for booklets IR20 and IR6.
Bank expatriate services can also help.
In France, information can be sought from the local Centre des Impôts (see telephone directory), or:
Centre des Impôts des Non Résidents
9 rue d'Uzès
75094 Paris Cedex 02
Tel: 1 42 36 02 33.

CHILDREN AND EDUCATION

Residence in France for children
In all the EC countries children are entitled to move and live with their parents as a matter of right. They will be granted residence when you apply for your Carte de Séjour.

Education
There are three options when going to live in France:

- Boarding school in the UK. This will result in separation of the family and it can be expensive. French employers will not usually pay toward this. Details of boarding schools in the UK are available from:
  Independent Schools Information Service (ISIS)
  56 Buckingham Gate
  London SW1E 6AG.
  Tel: (071) 630 8793.

- International schools in France. There are international schools in France which offer tuition partly or wholly in English. The

British School in Paris offers a totally British education and curriculum, and GCSE and A level examinations. French employers may pay these fees or pay towards them for executive level employees.

- Local schools. EC citizens can use state schools in France and this is free of charge. Simply approach your local school. There are very few private schools in France.

French education is to a high standard, but places more reliance on the desire of each student to study than in the UK. Few if any schools can offer help to those who do not speak French.

French qualifications (see Chapter 3) will soon be equivalent to those in the UK.

Higher education

All the French universities will usually accept UK students with A levels on an appropriate course of sutdy, but they may be required to undertake a language test. Tuition is not free.

A degree from a French university is recognised as having equal status with a UK one.

Further information

The Centre d'Information et de Documentation Jeunesse (CIDJ)
  101 quai Branly
  75740 Paris
  Tel: 1 45 66 40 20.
  Can provide information on higher education.

DAILY LIFE

Some other points worth considering before deciding to look for a job in France:

- Climate. France has four different climatic zones. The north-east is wet and cool, very much like the UK. The south is mild. The west is mild but wet, due to the influence of the Atlantic Ocean. In the east and other elevated areas it can be bitterly cold in winter.

- Clothes. Can you get clothing to suit your tastes locally? Generally, clothes are very expensive in France.

- Property. Is local property affordable and to your liking? Not all French property is bargain-priced.

- Furnishings. Much French furniture is highly modernistic, not traditional or even contemporary as in the UK. Is there anything you need or would like to take?

- Food. Food in France is excellent and cheap. However, not all British-type foods are available easily.

- Cost of living. Generally, lower than in the UK. Clothes and personal services can be costly. Costs very high in Paris.

- Travelling to work. Will you have to commute a long distance? How much will it cost? The French are becoming long distance commuters (some commute Lyon-Paris daily).

- Social life. It can be hard to meet people unless you speak French.

Plus, other matters which should not be taken for granted:

- Political situation. Reasonably stable, but a continual see-saw between Socialist and right-wing philosophy.

- Economic situation?

- Crime levels. High in some cities like Paris and Marseille and along the Côte d'Azur. Very low in rural areas.

- Personal freedom. Good, but police can be oppressive in some areas. French bureaucracy is formidable.

FURTHER HELP

- UK Embassies and Consulates. UK missions can only help with official matters (like passport renewals). Some will offer general help and advice to residents, but on an official basis. In an emergency they can help make arrangements, eg for hospitals or repatriation, but cannot pay for anything.

- Neighbours and colleagues at work. French people are usually pleased to help you if you ask (except perhaps in Paris). But ask in French!

- Other expatriates. Most French cities have a British expatriate community. There are also British expatriates on the Côte d'Azur, Normandy, Brittany, Aquitaine, etc. Ask the local

British Consulate or Office du Tourisme for a contact. There are also Anglican churches in some areas which will help.

- Tourist offices. A useful source of information and English-speaking help. Most tourist offices will be pleased to help foreigners, even if residents. An Office du Tourisme is a main tourist office, whereas a Syndicat d'Initiative is a small (often part-time) bureau.

- Police. Generally not willing to offer friendly help and advice, except perhaps in rural areas.

- Town hall. Occasionally you will find a friendly official at the mairie; most are officious and will enjoy tying you up with red tape!

- Clubs/newsletters. You might keep in touch with the expatriate life and issues with a club/newsletter like *Home and Away*.

7
Summing Up

A PLAN OF ACTION

Too many jobs?
As one of the largest industrialised countries in the world France undoubtedly offers a large number of opportunities. In some ways there are *too many* different opportunities and actual job vacancies, rather than too few. Foreigners can apply for all of these jobs—but there are certain types of job and types of industry where foreigners stand a much better chance of being employed. There are also jobs where it is an advantage to be a foreigner, rather than French, even in these days of a more united Europe.

A suggested approach
The best way to start is probably by narrowing down your options. Look at:

- specific industries you could work in;
- specific job opportunities;
- preferred areas of France;
- actual potential employers.

A narrower range of options will clarify the position.

A reminder
Remember that by and large the French do not go looking for foreign employees, although they are beginning to admit that they need to import foreign talent. In short, therefore, it is up to you to put yourself forward. Undertake some detective work to find potential employers. Contact them to sound out the possibilities. Make your abilities apparent. Merely waiting for advertised vacancies will lower your chances of success.

The crunch
Undoubtedly there are many jobs for foreigners in France and many

Summing Up

more coming up. Availability is not the problem, and skilled and experienced foreigners are largely insulated from much unemployment. The main problem is communication. This book has aimed to bridge the gap.

STEP-BY-STEP

1. Decide what job(s) you wish to do.

2. Decide which areas you prefer/are most appropriate.

3. Check for any vacancies in the UK newspapers.

4. Check for any vacancies in French newspapers.

5. Check relevant magazines, journals and bulletins.

6. Use the facilities offered by the UK Employment Service.

7. Use ANPE direct.

8. Use private employment agencies in both the UK and France.

9. Approach embassies, chambers of commerce, professional associations and trade directories for details of possible employers to which you may make speculative applications.

10. Consider the possibilities for a posting.

11. Make applications from the UK first.

12. If possible, consider travelling out to France on an exploratory trip.

13. Make applications on a continuous basis. If necessary return to first step and repeat procedure with other jobs and other areas.

14. Before accepting any job offer check out the practicalities of daily life: finding a home, health care, education, etc.

15. Accept job and travel to France.

Further Reading

BOOKS AND DIRECTORIES

The Au Pair and Nanny's Guide to Working Abroad, Susan Griffith and Sharon Legg (Vacation Work)
Business French (Collins)
Business French Made Simple, John Hudson and Nicole Tosser (Made Simple Books)
Buying a Home Abroad, Rebecca Stephens (Sidgwick & Jackson)
Careers Using Languages (Kogan Page)
The Daily Telegraph Guide to Working Abroad, Godfrey Golzen (Kogan Page)
The Directory of Jobs & Careers Abroad, Alex Lipinski (Vacation Work)
The Directory of Summer Jobs Abroad, (Vacation Work). New edition annually.
The Economist Guide: France (Hutchinson Business Books)
Emplois d'Été en France (Vacation Work) New edition annually.
France Today, John Ardagh (Penguin)
How to Get a Job Abroad, Roger Jones (How To Books, 2nd edition)
How to Get a Job in Europe, Mark Hempshell (How To Books)
How to Get That Job, Joan Fletcher (How To Books, 2nd edition)
How to Live & Work in France, Nicole Prevost Logan (How To Books)
How to Teach Abroad, Roger Jones (How To Books)
Opportunities in European Financial Services, 1992 and Beyond (John Wiley & Sons)
The Rough Guide Series: France (Harrap-Columbus)
The Single Market, The Facts (DTI)
Teaching English Abroad, Susan Griffith (Vacation Work)
Work Your Way Around the World, Susan Griffith (Vacation Work)
Working Holidays (Central Bureau)
Working in Ski Resorts – Europe (Vacation Work)

Further Reading

MAGAZINES AND JOURNALS

L'Entreprise (France)

L'Expansion (France)

Chapmans European Directory, Peter Kaye (Chapmans Publishers Ltd)

Connaught Executive Bulletin, 32 Savile Row, London W1X 1AG. Weekly bulletin of senior executive vacancies.

Courier Cadre, 8 rue Duret, F-75783 Paris. French directory of executive/professional job vacancies.

European Municipal Directory, Peter Kaye (Chapmans Publishers Ltd).

The Expatriate, First Market Intelligence Ltd, 56A Rochester Row, London SW1P 1JU. A monthly magazine covering matters of interest to the expatriate, with some vacancies.

Expatxtra, PO Box 300, Jersey, C.I. Monthly newsletter for expatriates with much information on financial matters.

Home & Away, Expats House, 29 Lacon Road, London SE22 9HE. Tel: (081) 299 4986. Monthly magazine covering expatriate matters with vacancies and an 'availability list' for members.

ICA Executive Search Newsletter, 3 rue d'Hauteville, 75010 Paris. Bulletin of senior executive vacancies.

Kompass Directories, (Kompass Publications). The Kompass directories (published for all main countries) are an authoritative list to industry in that country. Costly to purchase but should be available at all main libraries.

Nexus Expatriate Magazine, International House, 500 Purley Way, Croydon, CR0 4NZ. Tel: (081) 760 5100. Expatriate magazine with some job contacts (but largely biased to Middle East).

Overseas Jobs Express, PO Box 22, Brighton BN1 6HX. Tel: (0273) 440220. Bi-monthly newspapers for those seeking work overseas with 'Jobs' column.

Resident Abroad, 102-108 Clerkenwell Road, London EC1M 5SA. Tel: (071) 251 9321. Monthly magazine for expatriates giving much financial advice.

Single Market News, PO Box 1992, Cirencester, Glos GL7 1RN. DTI newspaper giving news of development towards the Single European Market. Useful background for job seekers.

1,000 Pistes de Jobs, 27 rue de Chemin-Vert, 75543 Paris. Bulletin of jobs, mostly suitable for students.

Useful Addresses

GENERAL ALPHABETICAL LISTING

Agence Nationale Pour l'Emploi, 53 rue Général Leclerc, 92136 Issy les Moulineaux. Tel: 1 46 45 21 26.
Assemblée Permanente des Chambres de Commerce et d'Industrie, 45 ave d'Iéna, 75016 Paris. Tel: 1 47 23 01 11.
Barclays Bank plc, Expatriate Dept, 13 Library Place, St Helier, Jersey. Tel: (0534) 26145.
Berlitz International, 79 Wells Street, London W1A 3BZ. Tel: (071) 637 0330. In Paris: 1 40 74 00 17.
British Association of Removers, 3 Churchill Court, 58 Station Road, North Harrow, Middx HA2 7SA. Tel: (081) 861 3331.
BUPA International Sales Office, Provident House, Essex St, London WC2R 3AX.
Central Bureau for Educational Visits and Exchanges, Seymour Mews House, Seymour Mews, London W1H 9PE. Tel: (071) 486 5101.
CEPEC Ltd, 67 Jermyn Street, London SW1Y 6NY. Tel: (071) 930 0322.
Christian Movement for Peace, Bethnal Green United Reformed Church, Pott Street, London E2 0EF. Tel: (071) 729 1877.
CIDJ (Centre d'Information et de Documentation Jeunesse), 101 quai Branly, 75740 Paris Cedex 15.
Commission of the European Communities, 8 Storey's Gate, London SW1P 3AT. Tel: (071) 973 1992.
Also:
9 Alva Street, Edinburgh EH2 4PH. Tel: (031) 225 2058.
4 Cathedral Road, Cardiff CF1 9SG. Tel: (0222) 371631.
9/15 Bedford Street, Belfast, BT2 7EG. Tel: (0232) 240708.
Council of British Independent Schools in the European Community, (COBISEC), Chaussée de Louvain, Tervuren, 1980 Brussels. Tel: (02) 767 47 00.
Department of Social Security (DSS) Overseas Branch, Newcastle Upon Tyne NE98 1YX.

Useful Addresses

DSS Child Benefit Centre (Washington), Newcastle Upon Tyne NE88 1AA.

Department of Trade & Industry, 1 Victoria Street, London SW1H 0ET. Tel: (071) 215 5000.

ECIS (European Council of International Schools), 21B Lavant Street, Petersfield, Hants GU32 3EW. Tel: (0230) 68244.

Employment Conditions Abroad Ltd, Anchor House, 10 Britten Street, London SW3 3TY. Tel: (071) 351 7151.

Employment Department, Qualifications and Standards Branch, Room E603, Moorfoot, Sheffield S1 4PQ. Tel: (0742) 594144.

Federation of Recruitment & Employment Services Ltd, 36-38 Mortimer Street, London W1N 7RB.

Inland Revenue Claims Branch, Merton Road, Bootle L69 9BL.

Institut Français, 14 Cromwell Place, London SW7 2DT. Tel: (071) 581 2701.

International Voluntary Service, 162 Upper New Walk, Leicester LE1 7QA. Tel: (0533) 549430.

Independent Schools Information Service (ISIS), 56 Buckingham Gate, London SW1E 6AG. Tel: (071) 630 8793.

L'Etudiant, 27 rue Chemin-Vert, 75543 Paris.

Linguaphone, 124 Brompton Road, London SW3 2TL.

Lloyds Bank plc, Isle of Man Expatriate Centre, 7-11 Douglas St, Peel, Isle of Man. Tel: (0624) 844051.

Manpower (UK) Ltd, 66 Chiltern Street, London W1M 1PR. Tel: (071) 224 6688.

Midland Bank plc, Expatriate Dept, 8 Library Place, St Helier, Jersey.

Natwest Expatriate Service, PO Box 12, 6 High Street, Chelmsford, Essex CM1 1BL. Tel: (0245) 261891.

Passport Office, Clive House, 70 Petty France, London SW1H 9HD.

Publicitas Ltd, 517-523 Fulham Road, London SW6 1HD. Tel: (071) 385 7723.

The Employment Service, Overseas Placing Unit, Steel City House, c/o Moorfoot, Sheffield S1 4PQ. Tel (0742) 596051.

United Nations Association, International Youth Service, Welsh Centre for International Affairs, Temple of Peace, Cathays Park, Cardiff CF1 3AP. Tel: (0222) 223088.

MAIN FRENCH REGIONAL NEWSPAPERS

Amiens: *Le Courrier Picard*, 29 rue de la République, 80010 Amiens Cedex. Tel: 22 82 60 00.

Angers: *Le Courrier de l'Ouest*, BP 728, boulevard Abert-Blanchoin, 49004 Angers Cedex. Tel: 1 40 12 07 77.

Angoulême: *La Charente Libre*, No. 3 Zone Industrielle, BP 106,

16001 Angoulême. Tel: 45 69 33 33.

Annecy: *L'Essor Savoyard*, 17 rue Sommellier, BP 65 74002 Annecy Cedex. Tel: 50 45 01 02.

Argenteuil: *Renaissance du Val d'Oise*, 2 boulevard Allemane, 95014 Argenteuil. Tel: 39 61 50 72.

Auxerre: *Yonne Républicaine*, 8-12 ave Jean-Moulin, BP 399 89006 Auxerre. Tel: 43 43 67 00.

Avignon: *Vaucluse Matin*, 4 rue de la République, 84000 Avignon. Tel: 90 82 32 80.

Bastia: *l'Informateur Corse*, 18 blvd Paoli, 20200 Bastia. Tel: 95 32 04 40.

Bordeaux: *Sud-Ouest*, 8 rue de Cheverus, 33000 Bordeaux. Tel: 56 90 92 72.

Bourg en Bresse: *Voix de l'Ain*, 6 bis rue de la Paix, BP 88, 01003 Bourg en Bresse. Tel: 46 05 04 03.

Bourges: *Le Berry Républicain*, 1-3 place du Berry, 18000 Bourges. Tel: 48 24 08 43.

Caen: *Liberté de Normandie*, 44 rue du Havre, BP 180 14015 Caen Cedex. Tel: 1 46 05 04 03.

Calais: *Nord Littoral*, 38 boulevard Jacquard, 62100 Calais. Tel: 1 46 05 05 06.

Cannes: *Avenir de la Côte d'Azur*, 13 boulevard Carnot, 06400 Cannes. Tel: 93 39 36 87.

Charleville: *L'Ardennais*, 36 cours Aristide-Briand, 08102 Charleville. Tel: 1 45 55 91 71.

Chartres: *L'Écho Républicain*, 39 rue du Chateaudun, BP 189, 28004 Chartres Cedex.

Clermont Ferrand: *La Montagne*, 28 rue Morel-Ladeuil, 63003 Clermont Ferrand. Tel: 73 34 20 08.

Dijon: *L'Avenir Hebdo*, 1 rue Saumaise, 21000 Dijon.

and:

Le Bien Public, 7 blvd Chanoine-Kir, BP 550, 21015 Dijon Cedex. Tel: 80 42 42 42.

Evreux: *La Dépeche*, 32 rue Doctor-Oursel, BP 425, 27004 Evreux Cedex. Tel: 32 33 00 89.

Grenoble: *Affiches de Grenoble et du Dauphiné*, 9 rue de New York, 38009 Grenoble. Tel: 76 96 21 42.

Ivry: *Nouvelles Val-de-Marne*, 4 rue Raspail, 94200 Ivry. Tel: 46 58 58 00.

Le Havre: *Havre Libre*, 37 rue Fontenelle, BP 1384, 76066 Le Havre Cedex.

Lille: *La Voix du Nord*, 8 place du Général de Gaulle, 59800 Lille. Tel: 20 76 40 40.

Useful Addresses

Limoges: *l'Echo du Centre*, 46 rue Turgot, 8700 Limoges.
and:
Le Populaire du Centre, rue du Général-Catroux, BP 54 87011 Limoges.
Lyon: *Le Progès*, 93 chemin de Saint-Priest, 69680 Lyons Chassieu Cedex. Tel: 78 90 81 88.
Mâcon: *Le Progrès*, 80 quai Lamartine, 71000 Mâcon.
Marseille, *Le Méridional*, 4 rue Cougit, 13001 Marseille. Tel: 91 84 45 45.
and:
La Provençal, 243 ave Roger-Salengro, BP 100, 13015 Marseille. Tel: 91 84 45 45.
Metz: *Le Républicain Lorrain*, 3 rue de Saint-Eloy, BP 89, 57014 Metz-Wolppy. Tel: 87 33 22 00.
Montpellier: *Midi Libre*, Le Mas de Grille, Saint-Jean-de-Védas, 34063 Montpellier Cedex. Tel: 67 07 67 07.
Mulhouse: *l'Alsace*, 24 ave Kennedy, BP 1199, 68053 Mulhouse Cedex.
Nantes: *Presse-Océan*, 7-8 allée Duguay-Trouin, 44010 Nantes Cedex.
Nice: *Nice Matin*, 214 route de Grenoble, BP23, 06021 Nice Cedex.
Nîmes: *Nîmes Journal*, 1 rue des Flottes, 30000 Nîmes. Tel: 66 67 53 22.
Pau: *La République des Pyrénées*, 49 rue Emile Guichenné, 64000 Pau.
Poitiers: *Centre Presse*, 5 rue Victor Hugo, 86000 Poitiers. Tel: 49 41 17 80.
Reims: *l'Union*, 87-91 place Drouet d'Erlon, 51083 Reims Cedex.
Rennes: *Ouest-France*, zone Industrielle de Rennes-Chantepie, 35051 Rennes Cedex. Tel: 99 03 62 22.
Roubaix: *Nord-Eclair*, 16-21 rue du Claire, 59100 Roubaix.
Rouen: *Paris-Normandie*, 19 place du Général-de-Gaulle, BP 563 76004 Rouen Cedex. Tel: 35 14 56 56.
Saint-Etienne: *Les Dépêches*, 16 place Drouet d'Erlon, 42000 Saint Etienne. Tel: 77 32 79 97.
Strasbourg: *Les Dernières Nouvelles d'Alsace*, 17 rue de la Nuée-Bleue, 67001 Strasbourg Cedex. Tel: 88 23 31 23.
Toulouse: *La Dépêche du Midi*, av Jean-Baylet, 31095 Toulouse Cedex. Tel: 61 62 62 11.
Tours: *La Nouvelle République du Centre-Ouest*, 232 ave de Grammont, 37048 Tours. Tel: 47 31 70 00.

Paris
France-Soir, 100 rue Réaumur, 75002 Paris. Tel: 1 40 01 20 00.
International Herald Tribune, 181 ave Charles-de-Gaulle, 92521 Neuilly. Tel: 1 46 37 93 00.
Le Monde, 15 rue Falguière, 75501 Paris Cedex 15. Tel: 1 40 65 25 25.

Le Figaro, 25 ave Matignon, 75398 Paris Cedex 08. Tel: 1 42 21 62 00.

CHAMBERS OF COMMERCE

Chambre de Commerce Française de Grande Bretagne Ltd, (French Chamber of Commerce in UK), Knightsbridge House, 197 Knightsbridge, London SW7 1RB. Tel: (071) 225 5250.

Midlands Chapter, Wilkes House, 41 Church Street, Birmingham, B3 2RT. Tel: (021) 212 1149.

Franco-British Chamber of Commerce, 8 rue Cimarosa, 75016 Paris.

Main French Chambers

Bordeaux: 12 place de la Bourse, 33076 Bordeaux. Tel: 90 91 28.

Grenoble: 6 boulevard Gambetta, 38028 Grenoble. Tel: 76 47 20 36.

Lille: place du Théâtre, 59000 Lille. Tel: 20 74 14 14.

Lyon: 20 rue de la Bourse, 69002 Lyon. Tel: 78 38 10 10.

Marseille: Palais de la Bourse, 13222 Marseille. Tel: 91 91 91 51.

Montpellier: 32 rue Grand rue Jean-Moulin, 83000 Montpellier. Tel: 67 55 91 55.

Nancy: 40 rue Henri-Poincaré, 54000 Nancy. Tel: 83 36 46 43.

Nantes: 16 quai Ernest-Renaud, 44000 Nantes. Tel: 40 20 90 00.

Nice: 20 boulevard Carabacel, 06000 Nice. Tel: 93 55 91 55.

Paris: 27 ave de Friedland, 75382 Paris. Tel: 1 42 89 70 00.

Rouen: 34 rue Bouquet, 76000 Rouen. Tel: 35 98 47 28.

Strasbourg: 10 place Gutenberg, Strasbourg. Tel: 88 32 12 55.

Toulouse: 2 rue d'Alsace-Lorraine, 31002 Toulouse. Tel: 61 25 21 00.

EMBASSIES AND CONSULATES

French Embassy, 58 Knightsbridge, London SW1X 7JT. Tel: (071) 235 8080.

French Consulate, PO Box 50, 21 Cromwell Road, London SW7 2EN. Tel: (071) 581 5292.

French Consulate, 523-525 Cunard Building, Pier Head, Liverpool L3 1ET. Tel: (051) 236 1156.

French Consulate, 11 Randolph Crescent, Edinburgh EH3 7TT. Tel: (031) 225 7954.

French Consulate, Philip le Feuvre House, La Motte Street, St Helier, Jersey, CI. Tel: (0534) 26256.

British Embassy, 35 rue du Faubourg St Honoré, 75008 Paris. Tel: 1 42 66 91 42.

British Consulate, 16 rue d'Anjou, 75008 Paris. Tel: 1 42 96 87 19.

British Consulate General, 15 cours de Verdun, 33081 Bordeaux. Tel: 56 52 28 35.

Useful Addresses

British Consulate General, 1 square Dutilleul, 59800 Lille. Tel: 20 52 28 35.

British Consulate General, 24 rue du Prado, 13006 Marseille. Tel: 91 53 43 32.

British Consulate General, 24 rue Childebert, 69288 Lyon. Tel: 78 37 59 67.

MANPOWER BRANCHES (SELECTED)

Bordeaux: 9 cours Alsace-Lorraine, 33000 Bordeaux. Tel: 56 44 56 04/ 56 51 69 69.

Cannes: 4 boulevard d'Alsace, 06400 Cannes. Tel: 93 39 70 82/93 38 56 58.

Clermont-Ferrand: 22 rue Georges Clémenceau, 63000 Clermont-Ferrand. Tel: 73 93 92 57.

Dijon: 6 boulevard Georges Clémenceau, 21000 Dijon. Tel: 80 74 00 74.

Grenoble: three offices including: 7 rue Saint Joseph, 3800 Grenoble. Tel: 76 43 05 82.

Lille: 281 boulevard Victor Hugo, 59000 Lille Tel: 20 54 55 45.

Lyon: 12 offices including: 31 avenue de Saxe, 69008 Lyon. Tel: 78 24 08 27. 16 cours Vitton, 69008 Lyon. Tel: 72 74 00 09.

Marseille: eight offices including: 96 rue de la République, 13002 Marseille. Tel: 91 91 09 22.

Montpellier: 23 boulevard Louis-Blanc, 34000 Montpellier. Tel: 67 72 36 72.

Nancy: four offices including: 223 avenue du Général Leclerc, 54000 Nancy. Tel: 83 56 29 56.

Nantes: 1 allée Cassard/Cours du 50 Otages, 40000 Nantes. Tel: 40 06 29 29/40 20 38 38/40 20 27 27.

Nice: 49 boulevard René Cassin, 06000 Nice. Tel: 93 18 04 04.

Paris: 41 offices including: 9 rue Jacques Bingen, 75017 Paris. Tel: 1 44 15 40 40.

PARIS EMPLOYMENT AGENCIES (SELECTED)

Central Intérim, 16 agencies in Paris (region) including: 150 avenue Champs Elysées, 75008 Paris. Tel: 1 43 59 01 90.

Contact Intérim, 156 rue Faubourg St Denis, 75010 Paris. Tel: 1 40 37 10 10.

Des Hommes Qui Travaillent, 189 avenue Gambetta, 75020 Paris. Tel: 1 43 63 63 53.

ECCO Travail Temporaire, 116 agencies in Paris (region) including: 33 rue Raffet, 75016 Paris. Tel: 1 45 25 21 21.

Manpower, 41 agencies in Paris (city) including: 9 rue Jacques Bingen, 75017 Paris. Tel: 1 47 66 03 03.
Minerve Intérim, 422 rue Saint-Honoré, 75008 Paris. Tel: 1 42 61 76 76.
IPB Travail Temporaire, 60 rue Ordener, 75018 Paris. Tel: 1 42 57 11 20.
Kelly, 50 avenue Champs Elysées, 75008 Paris. Tel: 1 42 56 44 88.
Permanence Européene, Avenue Kléber, 75116 Paris. Tel: 1 45 53 57 37 22.
and:
13 boulevard de Magenta, 75010 Paris. Tel: 1 42 03 34 08.
Most of the agencies listed deal in all types of work. The list comprises only a selection from several hundred temporary employment agencies in Paris. For a full listing, including details of agencies covering specialist occupations, refer to the Paris *Yellow Pages*.

MAJOR EMPLOYERS IN FRANCE

Aérospatiale, 37 bd de Montmorency, 75016 Paris. Tel: 1 42 24 24 24. Aerospace; aviation.
Air France, 1 square Max Hymans, 75015 Paris. Tel: 1 43 23 81 81. Air Transport.
L'Air Liquide, 75 quai d'Orsay, 75007 Paris. Tel: 1 40 62 55 55. Chemicals.
Béghin Say, rue Joseph Béghin, 59239 Thumeries. Tel: 20 62 44 00. Food processing.
Bouygues, 1 av Eugène Freyssinet, 78280 Guyancourt. Tel: 1 30 60 30 60. Construction.
BP, 10 quai Paul Doumer, 92400 Courbevoie. Tel: 1 47 58 40 00. Oil.
BSN, 7 rue de Téhéran, 75008 Paris. Tel: 1 42 99 10 10. Food processing.
Carrefour, 5 av du long Rayage, 91091 Lisses. Tel: 1 80 86 96 52. Retail sector.
Casino, 110 av Aristide Briand, 92120 Montrouge. Tel: 1 46 55 90 00. Distribution.
CEA Industrie, 31-33 rue de la Fédération, 75015 Paris. Tel: 1 40 56 10 00. Nuclear power.
CGE, 54 rue la Boétie, 75008 Paris. Tel: 1 40 76 10 10. Electrical manufacturing, télématique.
Docks de France, 21 av du Mennelos, 37000 Tours. Tel: 47 39 39 39. Docks.
Dumez, 345 av George Clemenceau, 92000 Nanterre. Tel: 1 47 76 42 43. Construction industry.

Useful Addresses

EDF, 2 rue Louis Murat, 75008 Paris. Tel: 1 40 42 22 22. Electricity utility.
Elf Aquitaine, 2 place de la Coupole, 92400 Paris. Tel: 1 47 44 53 69. Oil indusry.
ESSO-SAF, 6 av André Prothin, 92400 Courbevoie. Tel: 1 49 03 60 00. Oil industry.
FIAT, 140 av des Champs Elysées, 75008 Paris. Tel: 1 45 62 82 00. Motor industry.
France Télécom, 6 place d'Alleray, 75015 Paris. Tel: 1 44 44 22 22. Telecommunications.
Gaz de France, 23 rue Philibert Delorme, 75017 Paris. Tel: 1 47 54 20 20. Gas utility.
Générale des Eaux, 52 rue d'Anjou, 75008 Paris. Tel: 1 42 66 91 50. Water and energy utility.
Groupe Bull, 121 av de Malakoff, 75016 Paris. 1 45 02 90 90. Computing; informatique.
Hachette, 83 av Marceau, 75016 Paris. Tel: 1 40 69 16 00. Publishing industry.
IBM France, 5 place Vendôme, 75001 Paris. Tel: 1 49 05 70 00. Computing; informatique.
Imetel, 33 av du Maine Tour Mairie, 75015 Paris. Tel: 1 45 38 48 48. Metal industry.
Lafarge-Coppée, 28 rue Emile Menier, 75016 Paris. Tel: 1 47 04 11 11. Construction.
Michelin, place des Carmes, 63000 Dechaux. Tel: 73 30 42 21. Tyre manufacturing; publishing.
OCP, 24 rue des Ardennes, 75019 Paris. Tel: 1 40 03 45 25. Distribution.
L'Oréal, 14 rue Royale, 75008 Paris. Tel: 1 40 20 60 00. Cosmetics; pharmaceuticals.
Orkem, Tour Aurore, 92400 Courbevoie. Tel: 1 47 78 51 51. Chemicals industry.
Pechiney, 23 rue Balzac, 75008 Paris. Tel: 1 45 61 61 61. Metal industries.
Philips, 50 av Montaigne, 75008 Paris. Tel: 1 40 74 33 00. Electronics.
La Poste (PTT) 6 bd de la Marne, 76000 Rouen. Tel: 35 08 70 70. Postal services.
Le Printemps, 102 rue de Provence, 75009 Paris. Tel: 1 42 82 50 00. Retail sector.
PSA (Peugeot-Citroën), 75 av de la Grande Armée, 75016 Paris. Tel: 1 40 65 55 11. Motor manufacturing; engineering.
Promodès, route de Paris, 14120 Mondeville. Tel: 31 70 60 00. Distribution.

Renault, 18410 Argent sur Sauldre. Tel: 48 73 62 81. Motor manufacturing.
Rhône-Poulenc, 25 quai Paul Doumer, 92400 Courbevoie. Tel: 1 47 68 12 34. Chemical industry.
Saint Gobain, Les Miroirs, 92400 Courbevoie. Tel: 1 47 62 33 30. Glass manufacturing.
Schneider, 4 rue de Longchamp, 75016 Paris. Tel: 1 45 05 78 00. Electronics.
Shell France, 23-25 av de la République, 92500 Rueil Malmaison. Tel: 1 47 52 27 00. Oil industry.
SNCF, 88 rue St Lazare, 75009 Paris. Tel: 1 42 85 60 00. French state railways.
Système-U, 7 chemin de la Moselle, 57160 Scy-Charelles. Tel: 87 34 46 46. Distribution.
Thomson-CSF, 51 Esp du G de Gaulle, La Défense 10, 92800 Puteaux. Tel: 1 49 07 80 00. Electronics.
Total-CFP, 5 rue Michel Ange, 75016 Paris. Tel: 1 47 43 80 00. Oil industry.
Usinor-Sacilor, 4 place de la Pyramide, Défense 9, 92800 Puteaux. Tel: 1 49 00 60 10. Iron and steel.
Viniprix, 4 quai de Bercy, 94220 Charenton le Pont. Tel: 1 43 75 94 66. Distribution.

This listing comprises only a brief selection of France's largest companies and employers. For further contacts refer to the *Kompass France* directory.

MAIN UK COMPANIES IN FRANCE

British Airways, Tour Winterthur, 92085, Paris la Défense.
Barclays Bank, 33 rue du 4 Septembre, 75002 Paris.
British Steel France, 21 rue des Trois Fontanot, 92024 Nanterre.
Commercial Union Assurance, 104 rue du Richelieu, 75002 Paris.
Alfred Dunhill, 4 rue Roger Bacon, 75017 Paris.
Guardian Royal Exchange, 42 rue des Mathurins, 75008 Paris.
ICI France, 1 av Newton, 92142 Clamart.
ICL France, 24 av de l'Europe, 78140 Velizy.
International Westminster Bank, 18 place Vendôme, 75001 Paris.
Laboratories Fison, Chemin du Petit Bois, 69132 Ecuilly.
Laboratories Glaxo, 43 rue Vineuse, 75004 Paris.
Legal & General Assurance, 58 rue de la Victoire, 75009 Paris.
Lloyds Bank France, 43 bd des Capucines, 75002 Paris.
Marks & Spencer France, 6-8 due des Mathurins, 75008 Paris.
Midland Bank, 6 rue Piccini, 75116 Paris.
Reckitt & Coleman, 15 rue Ampère, 91301 Massy.

Useful Addresses

Rover Group France SA, rue Ambrose Croziat, 95101 Argenteuil.
Rowntree Mackintosh, Noisiel, 77422 Marne-la-Vallée.
Thorn EMI, 12-14 rue de l'Eglise, 75009 Paris.
Trusthouse Forte Hotels, 23 place Vendôme, 75001 Paris.
Wimpey, 72-78 Grande rue, 92310 Sevres.
WH Smith & Son, 248 rue de Rivoli, 75001 Paris.
This listing comprises only a small, representative sample of UK companies active in France.

UK EMPLOYMENT AGENCIES

Angel International Recruitment, Angel House, 50 Fleet Street, London EC4Y 1BE. Tel: (071) 583 1661.
James Baker Associates, 32 Savile Row, London W1X 1AG. Tel: (071) 439 9311. (Computer)
Sheila Burgess, The Power House, Alpha Place, Flood Street, London SW3 5SZ. Tel: (071) 351 6931. (Secretarial)
William Channing, Clarendon House, 11-12 Clifford St, London W1X 1RB. Tel: (071) 491 1338. (Banking/finance/industrial)
Eagle Recruitment, Eagle Place, 210-212 Piccadilly, London W1V 9LD. Tel: (071) 823 9233.
Electronics Recruitment Company, 32 North Street, Lewes, East Sussex BN7 2PQ. Tel: (0273) 480088. (Computer/electronics)
Forsyth, 87 Jermyn Street, London SW1Y 6JD. (Marketing)
Ingineur Ltd, Pendicke Street, Southam, Warwickshire CV33 OPN. Tel: (0926) 817612. (Electronics)
International Secretaries, 173 New Bond Street, London W1Y 9PB. (Secretarial)
Jenrick CPI Ltd, 140 High Street, Egham, Surrey TW20 9HL. Tel: (0784) 31411. (Computing)
Merton Associates Ltd, Merton House, 70 Grafton Way, London W1P 5LN. (Management)
Multilingual Services, 2 Charing Cross Road, London W1V 3TB. Tel: (071) 836 3794.
Track International, PO Box 292, High Wycombe HP13 5XS. Tel: (0494) 451692. (Computing)
Vision Appointments, Eastgate House, 16-19 Eastcastle Street, London W1N 7PA. Tel: (071) 631 4146.
These agencies are believed to deal in French vacancies, but no indication can be given as to the regularity with which suitable vacancies occur. Most can place only well qualified and experienced personnel.

There are bound to be other agencies which deal with French vacancies but which do not promote this. For a full list of all employment agencies refer to the *CEPEC Recruitment Guide*. For agencies dealing in nannying/au pair work and voluntary work refer to Chapter 5.

MAIN ANPE OFFICES

Bordeaux:
  1 terrasse Front du Medoc, 33000 Bordeaux. Tel: 56 00 18 00.
Grenoble:
  North: 17 rue Denfert Rocherau, 38000 Grenoble. Tel: 76 87 61 43.
  South: 23 rue Trembles, 38000 Grenoble. Tel: 76 40 72 61.
Lille
  63 rue Buffon, 59000 Lille. Tel: 20 85 15 40.
Lyon:
  98 rue Boileau, 69006 Lyon. Tel: 78 52 69 07.
Marseille:
  Bâtiment Chantepierre, 31 chemin Clue, 13011 Marseille. Tel: 91 43 04 38.
Montpellier:
  8 bis rue Castilhon, 34000 Montpellier. Tel: 67 58 59 70.
Nancy:
  12 place Croix de Bourgogne, 54000 Nancy. Tel: 83 27 46 62.
Nantes:
  12 avenue Carnot, 44000 Nantes. Tel: 40 48 48 48.
Nice:
  24 rue Edouard Béri, 06000 Nice. Tel: 93 62 29 68.
Paris:
  50 offices including: 10 rue Moulin des Pres, 75013 Paris. Tel: 1 45 80 05 60
Rennes:
  Agence Rennes Centre, 19 boulevard St Conwoin, 35000 Rennes. Tel: 99 35 13 13.
Rouen:
  29 rue Arsins, 76000 Rouen. Tel: 35 98 01 56.
Strasbourg:
  Centre Régional Alsace, 4 rue Sarrelouis, 67000 Strasbourg. Tel: 88 75 04 50.
Toulouse:
  5 offices including: 47 rue Balance, 31000 Toulouse. Tel: 61 62 42 38.

This listing represents only the ANPE offices in major cities. Details of other local offices can be found in the relevant French telephone directory.

Useful Addresses

CIDJ OFFICES

Nice:
  CIJ Côte d'Azur, Angle rue Delille, 19 Gioffrédo. Tel: 93 80 93 93.
Marseille:
  Cedex 04, CIJ Provence-Alpes, 4 rue de la Visitation. Tel: 91 49 91 55.
Caen:
  CIJ de Basse Normandie, 104 boulevard du Maréchal Leclerc. Tel: 31 85 73 60.
Dijon:
  CIJ Bourgogne, 22 rue Audra. Tel: 80 30 35 56.
Besancon:
  CIJ de Franche Comté, 27 rue de la République. Tel: 81 83 20 40.
Toulouse:
  CRIJ Toulouse Midi Pyrénées, 17 rue de Metz. Tel: 61 21 20 20.
Bordeaux:
  CIJ Aquitaine, 5 rue Duffour Dubergier and 125 cours Alsace-Lorraine. Tel: 56 48 55 50.
Montpellier:
  CIJ Languedoc-Roussillon, 190 avenue du Père Soulas. Tel: 67 61 12 00.
Rennes Cedex:
  CIJ Bretagne, Maison du Champ de Mars, 6 cours des Alliés. Tel: 99 31 47 48.
Grenoble:
  CRIJ Alpes-Vivarais, 8 rue Voltaire. Tel: 76 54 70 38.
Nantes:
  CRIJ des Pays de la Loire, 28 rue du Calvaire. Tel: 40 48 68 25.
Orléans:
  CRIJ région Centre, 18 rue des Bons-Enfants. Tel: 38 54 37 70.
Reims:
  CIJ Champagne-Ardenne, 41 rue de Talleyrand. Tel: 26 47 46 70.
Nancy:
  CIJ Lorraine, 20 quai Claude Le Lorrain. Tel: 83 37 04 46.
Lille:
  CRIJ Nord, Pas-de-Calais, 2 rue Nicolas Leblanc. Tel: 20 57 86 04.
Clermont-Ferrand:
  CIJ Auvergne, 8 place de Regensburg. Tel: 73 35 10 10.
Strasbourg:
  CIJ Alsace, 7 rue des Ecrivains. Tel: 88 37 33 33.
Lyon Cedex 02:
  CRIJ du Lyonnais, 9 quai des Célestins, BP 2308. Tel: 78 37 15 28.

Rouen
  CIJ de Haute-Normandie, 84 rue Beauvoisine. Tel: 35 98 38 75.
Melun:
  CIJ Seine-et-Marne, 36 avenue de la Libération. Tel: 1 64 39 60 70.
Versailles:
  Yvelines Information Jeunesse - CIJ des Yvelines, 48 avenue de Saint-Cloud. Tel: 1 39 50 22 52.
Amiens:
  CRIJ de Picardie, 56 rue du Vivier. Tel: 22 91 21 31.
Poitiers Cedex:
  CRIJ Poitou-Charentes, 64 rue Gambetta, BP 176. Tel: 49 88 64 37.
Limoges:
  CIJ du Limousin, Hôtel de Région, 27 boulevard de la Corderie. Tel: 55 45 18 70/71.
Evry Cedex:
  CIJ Essonne, 110 Agora, BP 102, Tel: 1 60 78 27 27.
Cergy Pontoise Cedex:
  CIJ du Val d'Oise, Parvis de la Préfecture, 1 place des Arts, BP 315. Tel: 1 30 32 66 99.

Glossary of French Employment Terms

ANPE, Agence Nationale Pour L'Emploi. French state employment agency.
ASSEDIC, Association pour l'Emploi Dans l'Industrie et le Commerce. Association for employment in industry.
Agences Locales et Antennes Saisonnieres. Seasonal employment offices.
APEC, Association Pour l'Emploi des Cadres. Employment bureau for executives.
Baccalauréat. Examination/qualification with similar status to A levels.
Brevet. Any type of certificate, but usually denoting a more prestigious academic one.
Bulletin de paie. Pay slip.
Caisse Primaire d'Assurance Maladie. Sickness insurance office, deals with most social security benefits. Also known simply as the Caisse or Caisse Primaire.
Centre d'Information et d'Orientation. Advice on public sector employment.
CIDJ, Centre d'Information et de Documentation Jeunesse. Information on education and employment for young people.
Cadre. An executive (with certain education/background).
Carte de Séjour. Residence permit.
Chambre de commerce. Chamber of commerce.
CIF. Statutory paid leave.
Comité d'entreprise. Works council.
Conseil des Prud'hommes. Industrial tribunal or labour court.
Contrat de travail. Contract of employment.
Convention collective. Collective agreement.
Délégué syndical. Shop steward.
Délégué du personnel. Personnel representative.
Demandes d'Emploi. Situations wanted.
Diplôme. Degree.

Grandes Ecoles. Prestigious universities (similar to Oxford/Cambridge).
Grève. Strike (industrial action).
L'inspection du travail. Labour inspector.
Horaire flexible. Flexitime.
Lettre de candidature manuscrite. A handwritten letter of application.
Loi Rondy dur l'Egalité Professionnelle. Equal Opportunities Act 1983.
Mairie. Town hall (where most administration is done and most licences/permits obtained).
Minitel. Computer information system.
Ouvrier qualifié. Skilled worker.
Ouvrier spécialisé. Semi-skilled worker.
Prime. Bonus (an incentive).
Régime de Retraite Sans Retenues. Non-contributory pensions scheme.
Responsable du personnel. Personnel manager.
Service du personnel. Personnel department.
SMIC, Salaire Minimum Interprofessionnel de Croissance. Index-linked minimum wage.
Syndicat. Trade union.
Système d'intérressement aux bénéfices. Profit sharing scheme (also known simply as intéressement).
Test d'aptitude. An aptitude or selection test.
Votre prétentions. Your expected salary.

Index

A levels, 54
Advertisements (situations wanted), how to write, 42
Aerospace industry, 101
Agence Nationale pour l'Emploi, see ANPE
Agences Locales et Antennes Saisonnières, 30
Agriculture, 101, 113-114
AJF, 111
ANPE, 25, 29, 30-31, 33
Service International, 48
APCCI, 45
APEC, 31
APECITA, 31
Application forms, 67-69
Applications, how to write, 59-64
Attitudes to employees, 54-55
Au pair work, 114-115

Baccalauréat, 52-53
Banking, finance, insurance, 102
Benn's Media Directory Europe, 42
Bonuses and benefits, 86-87

Cadre system, 90-91
Career bulletins, 21
Cars (company), 87
importing, 122-123
Carte de Séjour, 31, 36
Case histories, 17
Casual work, 109-118
Centre d'information et d'Orientation, 101
CEPEC Recruitment Guide, 35
Chambers of commerce, 44-45
Charity work, 115-117
Chemical industry, 103

Children and education, 134-135
CIDJ (Centre d'Information et de Documentation Jeunesse), 110
CIF, 82
Colleagues, dealing with, 88-89
Collective agreements, (conventions collectives), 80, 93-94
Conseil des Prud'hommes, 84, 88
Contract of employment (contrat de travail), 77-80
CROUS, 110
Curriculum vitae (CV), 62-67

Defence equipment industry, 104
Degrees (university), 54
Délégation à la Formation Professionnelle, 52
Demandes d'Emploi, 41, 43
Department of Trade and Industry (DTI), 52
Direction Départementale du Travail et de l'Emploi, 83
Direction des Journeaux Officiels, 94
Disciplinary procedures, 82-83
Dismissal, 82
Disputes at work, 83-84
Dossier, the, 68-69
Driving licences, 123

Economy, French, 12-13
Education, 134-135
Embassies and consulates, 44
Employment agencies, French, private, 35-37
Employment agencies, UK, private, 34-35
Employment agencies, UK, private, 34-35

Employment Department, Qualifications and Standards Branch, 51
Employment law, 76-84
Employment Service, the UK, 25
Employment Service, French, see ANPE
English language newspapers, 23
Envelopes (addressing), 65
Equality at work, 94-96
Ethnic minorities, 95-96
l'Etudiant, 45
EURES, 25
European Centre for Vocational Training (CEDEFOP), 49
European Certificate of Experience, 51
European Community (EC), 5, 11
Exchanges, working, 108-119
Expectations (of employers), 55-56, 89-90

First General System of Mutual Recognition of Qualifications, 50
Food processing industry, 104
France-Soir, 41
French Chamber of Commerce of GB, 40
French job advertisements, reading, 24-25, 26-28
French qualifications, 52-53
FRES Yearbook, 35

Grandes Ecoles, 53
GRETA, 82

Handwriting analysis, 57
Harmonised Training Directives, 49-50
Health and safety, 88
Health insurance benefits (from employer), 87
Hierarchy (in companies), 90
High-technology industries, 104
Holiday entitlement, 81
Holiday jobs, 109-118
Home, finding a, 125-127
Hospitals and health provision, 130-131

Income tax, UK and French, 132-134

Industrial disputes, see Strikes
Industrial tribunals, 84, 88
Industries, main French, 101-109, 118-120
Informatique, 105
l'Inspection du Travail (labour inspector), 82, 83
Insurance, 123
International recruitment network, 37-38
Interviews, 69-74
Iron, steel, aluminium industries, 105

Job titles, French, 25

Kompass France, 40

Language, learning, 124-125
Law, employment, see employment law
Letter of application, see Applications, how to write

Manpower UK Ltd, 37
Media, French, 21-23
Media, UK, 19-21
Migrations, 48
Minimum wage legislation, see SMIC
Mining, 106
Minitel, 37
Money and banks, 131-132
Motor industry, 106
Moving to France, 121-122

Nannying, 114-115
NATVACS, 29
Newspapers, advertising in, 41
Newspapers for jobs ads, France, 22
Newspapers for job ads, UK, 20
Notice (period of), 81

Old boy network, 19
Overseas Placing Unit (OPU), 29
Overtime, 81

Part time work, 83
Pay, 84-75
Pharmaceutical industry, 106
Photographs, 67

Index 159

Postings, securing, 45-48
Problems at work, dealing with, 88
Productivity bonuses, 86
Professional and executive jobs, 98
Professional associations, 44
Professional journals, France, 23-24
Professional journals, UK, 20-21
Profit sharing schemes, 86
Promotion, prospects for, 91
Property, purchase and rental, 126-127
Public employees, 83
Public sector, jobs in, 99-101
Publicitas Ltd, 42

Qualifications, 49-51
Qualifications (French), 52-53

Recruitment procedures, 56-59
Redundancy, 81-82
Referees, 67
Regions of France, 118-120
Residence in France, 75-76
Residence Permits, 75, see also Carte de Séjour
Retail sector, the, 107

Second General System, 50
Selection tests and techniques, 57-59
Semi-skilled jobs, 99
Shop stewards (délégué syndical), 83

Single European Market (SEM), 5
Skilled jobs, 99
SMIC (salaire minimum interprofessionnel de croissance), 81, 85
Social security, 127-130
Strikes, 94
SUPERVACS, 29

Tax, see Income Tax
Télématique, 107
Telephone directory, French, 32
Tourist Sector, the, 108, 112-113
Trades unions (Syndicats), 91-92
Training, 82

Unadvertised vacancies, 38-41
Unemployment, 13, 97
Unemployment benefits, France, 128
Unemployment benefits, transferring UK benefits, 129-131
Unskilled jobs, 99
Utilities industry, 109

Voluntary work, 115-117

Women at work, 94-96
Working conditions, 87-88
Working hours, 81
Works Councils (Comité d'Entreprise), 91-93